ASPECTS OF SOUTHERN STEAM

Stroudley 'Terrier' 0-6-0T No. 32661 in the process of 'running round' at Hayling Island, prior to returning with a service to the main line junction at Havant. *6th October 1959*
Unlike those other members of the 'A1X' Class to be seen in this album, all of which were saved from being cut up, No. 32661 – constructed in 1875 and rebuilt in 1912 – was withdrawn and scrapped in 1963.

'West Country' Class 'Light Pacific' No. 21C113 *Okehampton* had been in traffic for less than one year and was allocated to Exmouth Junction mpd when seen here. Still to receive nameplates (in June 1947), the locomotive was painted in the bright malachite green livery with three yellow horizonal bands. The fireman is taking a 'breather' from his efforts with the shovel, as this Up express – comprising at least eleven coaches – nears the end of the climb out of the picturesque Otter Valley. *28th September 1946*

Lightmoor Press

ASPECTS OF
SOUTHERN
STEAM

MIKE ARLETT & DAVID LOCKETT

For many years allocated to Plymouth Friary, Drummond Class 'T9' 4-4-0 No. 732 pulls away from Bere Alston with a lightweight stopping train, the (Sundays) 11.00am Plymouth to Exeter. *17th April 1938*
Dating from the very beginning of the 20th century, No. 732 entered service on the L&SWR in January 1900. Built by Dübs & Company at their Glasgow Works, No. 732 – the penultimate member of this famous class – had been superheated in 1927 and survived in service, as BR No. 30732, until withdrawn in October 1959.

FRONT COVER PICTURE: Photographed from the end of the Down platform at St. James Park Halt, 'Merchant Navy' Class No. 35022 *Holland America Line* accelerates up the grade away from Exeter Central with the 8.15am Plymouth (Friary) to Waterloo. *12th April 1954*
Norman's photograph was taken at that time of year (outside the period of the Summer Time Table) when this service included through carriages from both Torrington and Ilfracombe which, having been combined at Barnstaple Junction, were in turn added at Exeter Central to those from Plymouth.
Unlike the photograph on page 43, which features the same location, we must admit to the 'digital removal' of part of a very prominent telegraph pole to the left extremity of this view, which otherwise would have rather ruined an image selected to grace the front cover of this book!

REAR COVER PICTURE: Adams radial tank No. 30583 climbs across a high-arched accommodation bridge near Shapwick Green, with a Lyme Regis to Axminster train. The mid-winter sunshine reflects off the side of the solitary carriage (a Maunsell Corridor Composite Brake) which usually provided more than sufficient accommodation for the 'low season' traffic over this delightful branch line. *27th December 1960*

Previously published in The Norman Lockett Archive:
The Somerset & Dorset Railway 1935–1966, Mike Arlett & David Lockett, 2009, 2nd ed. 2010
Great Western Steam 1935–1949, Mike Arlett & David Lockett 2010
Western Region Steam 1950–1965, Mike Arlett & David Lockett 2011

Published by LIGHTMOOR PRESS
© Lightmoor Press, Mike Arlett & David Lockett 2015
Designed by Mike Arlett & Neil Parkhouse

British Library Cataloguing-in-Publication Data. A catalogue record for this book is available from the British Library

ISBN: 9781911038 03 0

LIGHTMOOR PRESS
Unit 144B, Lydney Trading Estate, Harbour Road, Lydney, Gloucestershire GL15 5EJ
www.lightmoor.co.uk
Lightmoor Press is an imprint of Black Dwarf Lightmoor Publications Ltd

Printed in Poland
www.lfbookservices.co.uk

CONTENTS

FOREWORD

In this, the fourth album of a series published by Lightmoor Press featuring 'The Norman Lockett Archive', we turn our attention briefly to the Southern Railway and then, in more detail, to its nationalised successor, the Southern Region of British Railways. However, it is only right we acknowledge that the contents of this album are very heavily biased in favour of the late 1950s and the 1960s, up until British Railways ended the use of steam motive power on the Southern Region in early July 1967. For that reason, unlike all three earlier books in this series, we decided to omit from the title any reference to the range of years (namely 1934-1967) from which we have selected images. Acting in the same vein, we have deliberately titled the book *Aspects of Southern Steam*, because the geographical coverage is not, by any stretch of the imagination, sufficiently wide-ranging to justify the more succinct title of 'Southern Steam'.

With the publication of this album (in late 2015), nearly eighty-two years will have passed since Norman Lockett commenced taking railway photographs. Some of the very earliest feature the former L&SWR main line on the western flank of Dartmoor, of which a selection are included herein. However, unlike his coverage of the GWR, Norman's photographs taken on the Southern Railway were much more limited in number during the period from 1934, when he commenced railway photography, until the outbreak of the Second World War, which brought an abrupt halt to his hobby. It is also evident that whereas, following the end of the war, Norman was frequently 'out and about' photographing GWR steam at lineside locations no more than a few miles from his home, his visits to photograph Southern Steam involved a lot more travelling during the period of immediate post-war austerity. Inevitably, therefore, there are less images featuring the latter which extended into the 1950s.

Whilst we have enjoyed working our way through the hundreds of glass plates in the Norman Lockett Archive to illustrate this album, we cannot deny a certain frustration (as was the case when preparing earlier books in this series) in discovering instances where the same few locations are featured time and time again. These include the western exit from Southampton Central (under that impressive signal gantry) and trains waiting to depart or setting off from Bournemouth West. Norman also took a great liking to locations either side (and particularly near the western portal) of Honiton Tunnel on the Salisbury to Exeter main line.

As might be expected, this album includes images of just a few examples of 'foreigners' who have strayed onto Southern metals (some associated with enthusiast's railtours) but only three featuring diesel locomotives!

We have continued with the format adopted for our earlier titles by presenting the content mostly in chronological order rather than on a geographical basis. One advantage is that this enables photographs of certain of Norman's favoured locations to be featured on two or sometimes several occasions. Even so, it has still proved possible to include only a small representation of those photographs featuring locations where he tended to take so many. The problem, therefore, has been which to select for inclusion

without over-exposure of such locations. However, as David recalls (and it is only right that we point out), the prime objective of his father – as was the case with several of Norman's contempories from his generation of railway photographers – was to create a better image than he had previously achieved at that same location.

Being a registered chemist and druggist from 1933, and a member of the Pharmaceutical Society, Norman's training served him well when it came to developing and making his own photographic prints. Railway photography might have been his hobby but the ethos of 'quality' was still the foremost – some might consider it almost an obsessive – aim. This has reminded Mike of a conversation held some thirty years ago with another fine railway photographer, Ivo Peters. On being asked by Mike which fellow photographer's work Ivo most admired, almost without a moment's hesitation he declared, "*Well, when it comes to quality, it must be my good friend Norman Lockett*".

Those who have purchased, begged, or borrowed earlier albums in this series will be aware that, until the mid-1950s, Norman relied entirely on public transport to get him and his heavy photographic equipment to the nearest possible location to where he intended to spend time by the lineside. This often involved a considerable 'hike' to some of the more remote places at which he had decided to spend perhaps less than an hour or, as was the case when travelling further afield from his home, for much of the day.

As David has previously recalled elsewhere, a trip as a youngster accompanying his father to Honiton involved a train from his home at Weston-super-Mare to Taunton, a bus from Taunton to the outskirts of Honiton, then a walk though the lanes to reach the lineside close to the western end of Honiton Tunnel. Later in the day, depending on the natural lighting and direction of the sun, a further walk might be undertaken across fields and along more narrow winding lanes to reach the cutting beyond the opposite end of the 1,345 yard-long tunnel. All this involved Norman carrying not only his quarter-plate camera but a back up camera as well, each in a stout leather case. One of these cases also included a storage pocket accommodating up to a dozen delicate glass plates, always Norman's preferred meduim for serious railway photography. So, here was another good reason why, having reached an acceptable or favoured location, Norman tended to 'stay put'. Even so, there were occasions when, having made all that effort to reach the lineside, just one or two glass plates were exposed. The reason was invariably an unexpected deterioration in the weather (lighting) conditions or the realisation that the location fell short of his expectations.

After relocating to Bath in 1957 and having struck up what became a lasting friendship with Ivo Peters (following a chance meeting at Bath Spa station the previous year), Norman gained the advantage of being chauffeured on joint photographic visits to linesides far and wide in Ivo's Bentley. Ivo, in turn, discovered a friend who was to prove a first class navigator! Both were members of the Bath Railway Society with whom visits were organised to motive power depots, private railway complexes, etc., on a regular basis. But it has to be acknowledged, whilst he found visits to depots and the like most enjoyable, when it came to serious photography, all the evidence suggests Norman invariably preferred to be out in the countryside, 'far from those madding crowds'; another trait he shared with Ivo.

Two Southern single track branch lines which were of particular appeal to both Norman and Ivo were those linking Havant to Hayling Island and Axminster to Lyme Regis. Both lines were worked by very elderly locomotives and, especially in the case of the latter named, provided a wide variety of photographic locations, despite it being just under 7 miles in length from the junction at Axminster. The two friends also visited the Isle of Wight on at least three occasions but appear to have spent most of their time on the busiest section between Ryde and Smallbrook Junction, where they could photograph – seemingly to their hearts' content – traffic serving the routes leading to Ventnor, and to Newport and Cowes.

So no apologies are made for the fact that such lines feature fairly heavily in this book.

As to another of Norman's favoured Southern branch lines, one wonders what he would have made of the fact that, more than sixty years after he first photographed 'the Purbeck Line', it is again possible to visit the same lineside locations to witness steam motive power taking the public, in large numbers, to and from the charming seaside town of Swanage. Doubtless he would have been most surprised but delighted to pay the occasional visit, complete with a compact digital camera and no longer faced with the prospect of having to spend very many hours each winter carefully developing glass plate negatives and producing large format prints.

Mike Arlett & David Lockett, 2015

ACKNOWLEDGEMENTS

In preparing the captions for this book, we wish to acknowledge Mike's use of the *Railway Observer* – the house magazine of the Railway Correspondence & Travel Society, *The Railway Magazine*, *Trains Illustrated* and *Railway World*. Likewise various websites, two of which deserve a specific mention; the Southern E Group (www.semgonline.com) and, discovered quite by chance, Six Bells Junction (www.sixbellsjunction.co.uk); the latter probably justified in claiming to be '*the home of what is very likely the largest archive of railtour information anywhere on the planet!*'

A growing number of books published by Irwell Press Ltd, each covering specific classes of Southern Railway steam locomotives or detailed histories of Southern lines to and around the West of England, have provided the source of much information. Details of all such titles can be found on their website (www.irwellpress.com).

Another title which has yielded much information about some favourite scenes photographed by Norman Lockett is *Southampton's Railways* by Bert Moody, published by Waterfront Publications.

When researching information about railways in and around Bournemouth and Poole, one can have no better a friend than a former Branksome (later Bournemouth) based engineman; Mike's many thanks go to Peter Smith.

As in earlier volumes, when it comes to queries regarding any signalling matters, Mike has turned to Chris Osment. Invaluable help has been provided by Brian Macdermott, who has responded to, or co-ordinated via his network of experts, various queries, often relating to coaching stock and engine duty numbers.

On looking through this book and (hopefully!) reading the captions, it will be very apparent that Norman shared his enthusiasm for railway photography with Ivo Peters. In the knowledge that the two men were often at the lineside together during the final decade of Southern Steam, Mike has been able to turn to Ivo's notes to check details. Our thanks to Julian Peters, who is now the copyright owner of his late father's photographs and films, and who – 'just for a bit of fun' – also allowed the inclusion of a photograph taken by Ivo on the same occasion and featuring the same scene as one taken by Norman (see page 61).

Except where noted otherwise, all text and captioning has been prepared by Mike who, as before, makes no claims as to originality of information other, perhaps, than in relation to some of the asides which, it is hoped, might add a little to your enjoyment of this book. In most cases, information is based on and enhanced from notes made by the photographer. Should there be any errors which have crept in regarding locomotive allocations, repairs, dates and the like, these will – we suspect – be down to Mike rather than those from whom he has sought information!

Norman Lockett, in the garden of his home in Bath. In addition to photography, he was a keen gardener and, somehow, also found time to follow the fortunes of Somerset Cricket Club, of which he was an ardent supporter. Quite an achievement during an era when his working week comprised up to 48 hours spread over 5½ days.

Norman noted the lighting conditions as 'brilliant' at the time (2.25pm) he photographed Class 'T9' 4-4-0 No. 714 approaching Wortha Mill Bridge in charge of the 8.40am Waterloo to Plymouth service.
29th May 1934

This was the scene northwards from 'Bridge No. 640'. Wortha Mill Farm stands immediately to the right (the rear corner of just one building can be seen cloaked with ivy). The impressive rock outcrop, Brent Tor, which rises to 1,100ft above sea level and is surmounted by the small 13th century St Michael's Church, stands barely a mile due west. The single line just visible on the extreme left, running at a slightly lower level, was the GWR's Plymouth-Launceston Branch. This paralleled the SR tracks for more than four miles from Lydford to the northern outskirts of Tavistock. The narrow watercourse separating the two routes is the infant River Burn (a tributary of the River Tavy). Perhaps it was the two parallel systems which had attacted Norman here? If so, he failed to record the passage of a single GWR train and never paid a return visit.

SECTION 1
1930s

Having only recently married and moved from his home town (Weston-super-Mare, in Somerset) to live and work in Plymouth, Norman Lockett appears to have taken his first railway photograph at Hemerdon Incline, at the start of April 1934 (see *Great Western Steam 1934-1949*, the second album in this series featuring 'The Norman Lockett Archive'). Less than two months later, on the 29th May 1934, he took his camera to the lineside of the Southern Railway for the first time. The result was the photographs opposite and below.

Why Norman decided to visit the somewhat remote location at Wortha Mill Farm, about half a mile south of Brentor station on the western flank of Dartmoor, is unrecorded. One can only speculate that, reliant on public transport for such 'expeditions', he had travelled out from his new home by train or bus, before walking to this location. We have often been surprised at how much walking Norman was prepared to undertake to reach some of the more rural lineside locations which he appeared to favour. David Lockett recalls that his father invariably pre-planned his routes, explaining: "*He excelled in reading bus and railway time tables, and Ordnance Survey maps, and was able to plan what appeared to me – all those decades ago – the most complex of journeys.*"

This, the second of Norman's photographs taken at Wortha Mill, shows another Class 'T9', No. 280, being the first example of the second batch built in 1899. This was an Exeter to Plymouth Friary train, which included a through coach attached to the rear. Brentor station was sited farther around the reverse curve beyond the rear of the train. Some houses fronting the road linking the station with the village (North Brentor) can just be made out in the left far distance.

WADEBRIDGE

In the summer of 1934, Norman paid a visit to Wadebridge. Unfortunately, the glass plate negatives have deteriorated badly and this is the only image which warrants reproduction. Beattie well tank 2-4-0 No. 329 was subsequently renumbered by the Southern Railway into the 'reserve' list as No. 0329 and was one of three of this class which survived until December 1962, in use on the lightly laid branch line to Wenford Bridge. Dating from 1875, No. 0329 had been reboilered in 1929 but – at the time of Norman's visit – still retained the original stovepipe-pattern chimney. Soon after this, the locomotive was renumbered again, as 3329, by the SR and, when later placed into BR stock, became No. 30586. She was destined to be the only one of the last working trio to be cut up for scrap after being withdrawn from service.

DEVONPORT

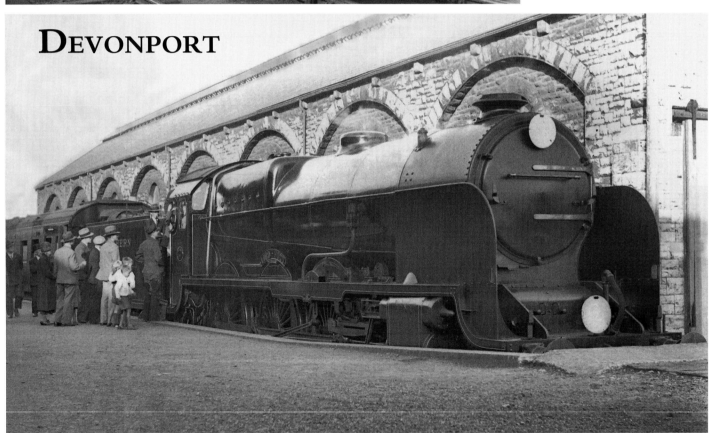

Despite living in Plymouth from 1934 and able to pursue his new-found hobby until interrupted by the outbreak of the Second World War, Norman all but ignored photography within the boundaries of the 'three towns' which formed the City of Plymouth. This, perhaps, reinforces the belief that, whenever time allowed, he much preferred rural locations in the pursuit of his hobby. However, an event which did draw him to Devonport station was the arrival of 'Lord Nelson' Class 4-6-0 No. 859 *Lord Hood*, which was placed on view for public inspection from 7th to 9th August 1934 as part of the annual 'Navy Week' celebrations. A weight restriction, barring use of this class on the Southern main line west of Exeter, resulted in the locomotive having to be brought from and returned to Exeter via the GWR route.

It was recorded that nearly 2,000 visitors turned up to inspect an immaculate No. 859. Just a few can here be seen awaiting their turn to climb on to the footplate. Who were the most excited – the children or the fathers? The location is the dock alongside the large goods shed at Devonport station and the exhibition arranged by the SR also included various items of modern coaching stock and goods vehicles.

PLYMOUTH FRIARY MPD

Another 'one-off' by Norman was his visit to the motive power depot at Friary on 15th March 1938. This is the view looking north-eastwards towards Friary Junction, featuring 'N' Class 2-6-0 No. 1831, with the south side of the shed forming the backdrop on the left. The main running lines are beyond the far (north) side of the shed.

Taken on the same side of the depot, this includes a partial view of the original hoist. Adams 'B4' Class 0-4-0T No. 103 dated from December 1893. These short-wheelbase locomotives were designed specifically for shunting various dockside and associated lines served by the former London & South West Railway (L&SWR). This example was withdrawn by BR in May 1949 and sold. The *Railway Observer* referred to the locomotive having been loaded onto a road trailer in Exeter Central Goods Yard on 27th May 1949 and it was later seen being transported through Taunton *en route* to Newcastle. No. 103 was sold to the Directorate of Opencast Coal Production, which had been transferred to the Ministry of Fuel & Power in 1945, and was sent to the Blue Bell site at Backworth in Northumberland still with its old number. It was dispatched to Robert Stephenson & Hawthorns for repairs in May 1953 but must have been beyond salvage, as it is recorded as being scrapped three months later. *15th March 1938*

HEADING TOWARDS DARTMOOR

Class 'U1' 2-6-0 No. 1900 with the 9.30am Plymouth-Brighton heads up the incline near Bere Ferrers. The locomotive, the last of a batch built at Eastleigh in 1931, entered service as No. A900 and had been allocated to Fratton. Neither David nor I have been able to establish the exact whereabouts of this location. *28th March 1937*

In charge of a Plymouth-Exeter service, Class 'T9' 4-4-0 No. 718 climbs northwards from Bere Alston through some delightful but windswept countryside, which rises from the Tamar Valley towards the south-western flank of Dartmoor. *Date in 1937 unrecorded*

As with the other examples of these 4-4-0s photographed by Norman around this locality, No. 711 is paired with a Drummond 8-wheeled 'watercart' tender. The location, near Rumleigh, to the north of Bere Alston village, can be confirmed by reference in the background to Calstock Viaduct. This carried the branch line to Callington (now truncated to Gunnislake) high across the River Tamar. *11th September 1938*

Having completed a 1 in 75 climb away from Tavistock station, 'U' Class 2-6-0 No. 1831 is able to take advantage of the now falling gradients and accelerates a Plymouth-bound train high above the roofs of the bungalows in Bolt House Close. The house prominent on the left, above the cutting, is still easily recognisable eight decades later and stands off the New Launceston Road. *16th September 1936*

Proposals are currently (2015) under consideration to reinstate a further 5½ miles of this railway, using the former trackbed between Bere Alston and the outskirts of Tavistock. This will enable Tavistock to be linked by rail to Plymouth for the first time since 1968. There is a further proposal to rebuild what would then be the missing link between Tavistock and Okehampton, recreating the old L&SWR line between Exeter and Plymouth, as there is a need for a second route through Devon to safeguard services against problems along the South Devon sea wall between Dawlish Warren and Teignmouth.

Norman was rather economic with some of the details relating to these early photographs. He described this location as '*on Honiton Bank*'. Featuring an Up train, this scene must be on the section leading east from Honiton station towards the western portal of Honiton Tunnel (the number of the telegraph insulators and layout of the cross members affixed to the lineside post in comparison with other photographs of this part of the main line would appear to confirm this). The train is the Up 'Atlantic Coast Express' (the 'ACE') hauled by N15 'King Arthur' Class 4-6-0 No. 747 *Elaine*. *11th August 1935*

THE 'ACE' AND THE 'BRIGHTON'

Ten minutes after the passage of No. 747 (above), Norman photographed another 'Arthur', No. 449 *Sir Torre*, in charge of a relief to the Up 'ACE'. He then walked out into the adjacent field where, just a further 10 minutes later, at 1.30pm, he was rewarded with this view of a third 'N15'; No. 457 *Sir Bedivere*, with the Plymouth-Brighton through train. *11th August 1935*

PASSING MOORCOX FARM

'H15' Class 4-6-0 No. 333, as rebuilt in 1924, tackles Honiton Bank with empty stock which appears to include several vehicles straight out of the paint shop. This photograph has been published before but only from a print made by Norman. It is included here as a good example of the advantages of scanning digital images direct from the original glass plates, by which we get to see the parts Norman would not have included in any print he made from his negative. *27th August 1935*

In this scene, most of the left half of this image was excluded when Norman made a print. By so doing, several clues to assist identification of the exact location around eighty years later were omitted. The boundary hedgerow with telegraph poles on the far side of the line suggested the probability of a track or roadway, leading (perhaps) from an overbridge to the group of buildings seen abutting the Up side of the line. In the left bottom corner (and out of focus!) is a concrete post and sloping fence-wire (again suggesting the proximity of a bridge). The back of a gradient post is visible. The profile for this section of Honiton Bank shows only one change of gradient immediately preceding an overbridge. A quick check using 'Google Earth' plus reference to the 'Bridge List' confirms this location as Ivy Green Bridge (No. 461) which carries Wilmington Lane over the line and past Moorcox Farm; the latter instantly recognisable as the buildings which feature in Norman's photograph.

'N15' Class 4-6-0 No. 448 *Sir Tristram* ascends the bank with a lightweight load, a Salisbury-Exeter stopping train. Norman recorded the time as 4.30pm so any reader with a *Summer 1935 Time Table* should be able to work out which train he photographed! *27th August 1935*

If Norman made a print of this image, it cannot now be found. However, as a comparison to that of No. 333 above, this – most likely – is how he would have made a print using less than the full width of that included on the glass plate. Having now identified the location, the overbridge just visable in the distance can be confirmed as that carrying what was (then) the A373 – later upgraded and redesignated as the A35.

A LAST PRE-WAR VISIT TO HONITON

The three photographs on these two pages were taken on Friday 9th June 1939 and were to prove Norman's last featuring Southern Railway steam prior to the outbreak of the Second World War, just three months later. Following this visit, eight years were to pass before he returned to the lineside hereabouts.

'U' Class 'Mogul' No. 1792 makes light work with an Up stopping service which comprised a 3-coach ex-L&SWR set. This locomotive had been rebuilt in 1928 at Eastleigh from 'River' ('K') Class 2-6-4T No. A792 *River Arun. 9th June 1939*

'N15' Class No. 788 *Sir Urre of the Mount* attacks the lower part of the bank east of Honiton with the Up 'Atlantic Coast Express'. The bridge in the background, we think, carried the A373 (as it was then designated) and the signal which can be seen was subsequently resited to the opposite (Down) side of the line. *9th June 1939*
The interruption to the running of this titled train during the war brought to an end the regular use of the 'King Arthur' Class on this service. When the title was reintroduced in October 1947, the task was assigned to the Bulleid 'Pacifics' which, in the intervening years, had been brought into service in increasing numbers.

Other than the date and time, the only other information Norman recorded was that this image shows 'King Arthur' Class No. 451 *Sir Lamorak* heading a Down train near Honiton. However, the layout suggests this scene is west of Honiton station, with the bridge in the background (No. 477) carrying the A375 to Sidmouth over the line and the Honiton Up Distant signal positioned to this side of it. Later, as Honiton expanded westwards, the land beyond the lineside hedge to the left would be developed for light industry and that to the right for housing. *9th June 1939, 3.10pm*

'Merchant Navy' Class No. 21C3 *Royal Mail* with an Up express crosses Northcote Hill Bridge – carrying the railway over the aptly-named Tunnel Lane – on the final approach to the western portal of Honiton Tunnel and the summit of the eastbound climb out of the Otter Valley. *28th September 1946*

No. 21C3 was released into traffic during September 1941, five years before Norman Lockett took this photograph, and is seen here with short flared-pattern smoke deflectors. First allocated to Salisbury, the locomotive transferred to Exmouth Junction the following autumn. Although repainted in wartime black in 1943, Royal Mail reverted to Malachite green livery during a visit to works in May 1945. The diagonal thin stripe across the 'top left-quarter of the smokebox door was created momentarily by a ray of sunlight penetrating the small gap behind the top of the deflector plate.

SECTION 2
THE LATE 1940S

Norman Lockett recommenced photographing Southern Railway steam just a few hundred yards from where his last pre-war shots were taken, some eight years and four months earlier. At first glance there was little apparent change, with locomotives and rolling stock much the same as pre-war. So we imagine there must have been at least a tinge of excitment when Norman captured an image of one of Mr Bulleid's 'Pacifics' powering up the bank. Whether any initial excitement waned as more and more examples of these locomotives, including the 'Light Pacific' varients, appeared in the viewfinder of his camera is a matter for conjecture!

The images shown on these two and the following few pages serve as a good example of Norman's tendancy to 'stay put' once he had discovered or revisited a location to his liking and to fire off the shutter until all the glass plates he carried that day had been exposed. As mentioned in the 'Foreword' to this book, the same propensity can be seen with other railway photographers of Norman's era, many of whom were exponants of the 'three-quarter front' view, perhaps the best recalled of whom is Maurice Earley. What appears evident is that such photographers were determined (as their primary objective) to achieve the finest, techanically correct, image possible. Hence the comment made to this writer by Ivo Peters (to which reference has also been made in the 'Foreword') regarding his friend Norman Lockett and the *quality* of his photographs.

There is little doubt in the opinion of the writer of these notes, that the use of photographic glass plates provided the best opportunity to create high quality prints and (more recently) from which superb digital images can be produced.

'King Arthur' Class 'N15' 4-6-0 No. 452 *Sir Meliagrance*, with original Drummond-style 'watercart' tender, climbs the 1 in 90 gradient towards the tunnel with an express bound for Waterloo. *4th October 1947*

Another of the 'King Arthur' Class, No. 789 *Sir Guy*, with a heavily loaded multi-portioned Up train. *28th September 1946*

A three-coach local was hardly a match for Drummond 'Greyhound' 4-4-0 No. 710, a Class 'T9' 4-4-0 dating from 1899. *28th September 1946*
The early bright weather conditions on this post-war Saturday had given way to an overcast sky. Deteriorating light often led to Norman abandoning photography for the remainder of the day – or returning much closer to home, in the hope that conditions might improve again.

A long-time allocation to Salisbury mpd, No. 452 *Sir Meliagrance* was a regular performer on some of the heaviest services over this route. Here, however, was a lighter loading for what was probably a service bound for Yeovil or Salisbury. Norman recorded the time (11.50am DBST – Double British Summer Time) but no other details. *27th July 1947*
Having spent several hours here photographing the succession of Up trains and with the position of the sun moving across the sky into the west, all Norman had to do was turn around and photograph whatever next appeared into view in the Down direction. This provided a seemingly endless procession of trains, each having just emerged from Honiton Tunnel. Little wonder he returned here many times!

Many might argue that, post-World War Two, there was no finer sight on the Southern than a Bulleid 'Pacific', still appearing much as originally built, sporting Malachite Green livery, and complete with brightly coloured headboard and 'Devon Belle' wingboards, in charge of a rake of Pullman coaches. No. 21C3 *Royal Mail* approaches the western portal of Honiton Tunnel with the Up 'Devon Belle'. *27th July 1947*
No. 21C3 had only regained its Malachite Green livery the previous winter, this replacing the war-time black carried since the spring of 1943. In 1950, it was repainted again, in the British Railways blue livery.

'THE DEVON BELLE'

During the same lineside visit, Norman also photographed the Down 'Belle' but did not have time to note the identity of this 'Merchant Navy'; perhaps a little too close for comfort as certainly his presence had been spotted by the driver! The locomotive had to be one numbered from 21C3 to 21C10, as these were the only members of the class with the horizontal stiffening rib at mid-height along the length of the 'air-smoothed' lightweight cladding. *27th September 1947*
Notice, on the extreme left side, some wooden framework. This was probably the remains of a temporary signal box, Honiton Tunnel West, in use from January 1899 to May 1902, when single line working was employed though the tunnel to a similar box at the eastern end. This enabled major repairs to be undertaken to a half-width of the tunnel at a time, whilst allowing traffic to continue to run. It was a similar arrangement as implemented more than a half-century later when Buckhorn Weston Tunnel required major repairs (see page 28).

Moving forward a couple of years by which time – despite appearances here – the railways had been Nationalised for more than eight months. No. 21C10 *Blue Star* brings the Down 'Belle' over the summit, immediately outside the tunnel mouth, and commences the long downhill section which continues (other than the passage through Honiton station) until the River Otter is crossed some 5½ miles farther west. *15th August 1948*

This member of the class was given its BR number, 35010, in time for the launch of the BR era but otherwise retained Southern Railway livery until November 1949, when it was painted in BR blue.

Missing a bit! No. 21C4 *Cunard White Star* climbs Honiton Incline with a Down express. *4th October 1947*
Note the locomotive is missing a deflector plate (or at least the forward section which projected ahead of the smokebox). It is the only occasion this writer can recall seeing any Bulleid 'Pacific' working in this condition. Also evident, the locomotive appears to have last been cleaned when still carrying the 'Devon Belle' wingboards!

'U' Class 2-6-0 No. 1618 with a Salisbury to Exeter service. *4th October 1947*
Taken at 4.53pm BST, this was the last photograph of a Southern Railway train that Norman took before the railways of Britain were Nationalised. Perhaps it was appropriate that it turned out to be a locomotive destined to escape being cut up, having been withdrawn from service in January 1964 and sold for scrap to Woodham Brothers at Barry. Rescued in January 1969 and only the second locomotive to leave Barry, No. 31618 was given to the Bluebell Railway and placed on a fifty year loan to the Maunsell Locomotive Society. Having been fully restored and run on the Bluebell Railway, the 2-6-0 is currently (2015) 'out of ticket' and on display in the running shed at Sheffield Park, awaiting the next overhaul.

A conversion to the 'H15' Class, 4-6-0 No. 30334 is seen hauling what Norman referred to as '*a West of England to Waterloo*' service. Note the earliest version of the British Railways livery on the 8-wheeled tender. *15th August 1948*
Rebuilt to the design of Urie, this 4-6-0 was brought back into traffic at the beginning of 1925, as one of the much more successful 'H15' Class. The locomotive was withdrawn in June 1958.
The glass plate of this image had deteriorated (or was faulty when first processed by Norman) but our publisher has done his best to remove the worst effects of a vertical band which had become much darker than the remainder of the image. However, photographs by Norman of these impressive rebuilds of the Drummond 'F13' Class (dating from 1905) are rare; hence its inclusion here.

Urie Class 'S15' 4-6-0 No. 30846, allocated to Exmouth Junction shed, heads westwards with a Down freight along a section of track which is level for just over a mile. This view is from a position about three-quarters of a mile north-east of that featured opposite, with the Millborne Port Up Distant signal visible to the left. *14th October 1950*

SECTION 3

MOVING FORWARD INTO THE 1950S

WEST OF MILBORNE PORT

Moving forward into the 1950s, we feature first some new locations sought out by Norman. The photograph below was taken about 1¼ miles south-west of Milborne Port station, looking in the direction of Sherborne and at the end of a 4¼ mile climb which lifts the main line out from the Yeo Valley. Just out of picture, to the left, is an occupation overbridge (No. 337), which leads from a lane linking Milborne Wick to the

A30 road near Crackmore (east of Sherborne). Norman described his picture somewhat vaguely as taken '*near Milborne Port*' and the exact location has been established with the help of Google 'Street View' and their little yellow 'Pegman'. The clue was that pair of telegraph poles; some 6½ decades later, the poles (or more likely their replacements) are to be seen in much the same position.

'West Country' No. 34042 *Dorchester* **had just breasted the summit of the eastbound climb with an Up train, most of which was still on the incline, the gradient having eased earlier to 1 in 200, after a gruelling stretch of more than a mile at 1 in 80.** *14th October 1950*
Just four years in traffic and based at Salisbury since spring 1948, No. 34042 had been renumbered into the BR system. The former 'Southern Railway' ownership, as originally displayed on both sides of the tender, had been painted over. The cab front had been modified in April 1949 but the original Malachite Green livery, complete with the yellow horizontal bands, would remain until repainted into BR livery late in 1951. In May of that year, this 'light Pacific' would be reallocated to Bath (71G) to work over the Somerset & Dorset Line. Although reallocated again, No. 34042 could still be seen working between Bournemouth and Bath, more often than not on busy summer Saturdays, until the through traffic ceased in 1962. She was rebuilt in the winter of 1959.

BUCKHORN WESTON TUNNEL – THE EASTERN END

Class 'S15' 4-6-0 No. 30846 features again, this time with an Up freight and having toiled up the 1 in 100 gradient through the 742 yard-long Buckhorn Weston (sometimes referred to as Gillingham) Tunnel. The summit here – very pronounced when seen as in this low-level shot – heralds the end of an eastbound climb of a little over 2 miles. Next come grades which favoured the locomotive, for a distance of about 2½ miles to Gillingham. *17th June 1952*

As evident by the water in the lineside cess, this was a relatively wet area which, over many decades, created problems within the confines of the tunnel. By the mid-1950s, both the tunnel invert and brick linings had so deteriorated that it became necessary (between 1958-61) to renew the floor with reinforced concrete and undertake major repairs to the brickwork. This required single-line working so, one at a time, the tracks through the tunnel were removed to enable the work to proceed first along one half-width, then the other. Temporary crossovers were provided at both ends to enable the passage of trains to continue.

Rebuilt 'Merchant Navy' Class No. 35018 *British India Line* lifts the 'ACE' the final 200 yards to the summit of the climb from Gillingham, the last mile of which was graded at 1 in 100. Only four months had elapsed since Nine Elms-based No. 35018 had been released back into traffic following modification – hence the immaculate condition of the locomotive witnessed here.

In contrast and just ten minutes later (with the sunshine having broken through the clouds), No. 35005 *Canadian Pacific* appeared with a relief to the preceding 'ACE'. Here in BR green livery, this member of the Class would be rebuilt during April/May 1959.

These two photographs were taken on Saturday 30th June 1956 and feature Down express trains. This is the same location as featured on the previous page but now looking in the opposite (easterly) direction. The lineside gang had been busy cutting back both sides of the cutting – a task yet to be fully completed on the Up side. The overbridge (No. 311) carries a minor road close to the merging of several lanes and stands about a mile west of the hamlet of Bugley.

CHRISTCHURCH

'Lord Nelson' Class 4-6-0 No. 30864 *Sir Martin Frobisher* eases what Norman recorded as a Bournemouth to Newcastle through train around the curve, which was subject to a speed restriction, just to the east of the station. The elevated signal box was sited immediately to the west of the bridge carrying Fairmile Road across the line. The tracks seen to the right (bounded by a row of WW2 'tank traps') had served as the original route from Ringwood. This had been closed to traffic in 1935 but a short length was retained at this end for use as sidings. *23rd July 1953*

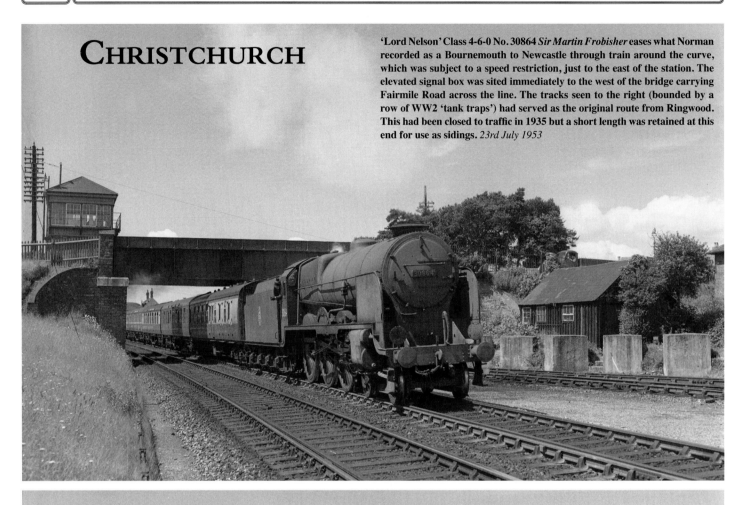

'West Country' No. 34005 *Barnstaple*, in charge of a Waterloo-Bournemouth West express, passes Pickfords furniture depository (subsequently demolished) at the western end of the station. Norman failed to record full details but note that the roofboards on the leading Bulleid corridor stock were reversed, with the lettering obscured. *23rd July 1953*
No. 34006 was one of the three 'light Pacifics' selected by the Southern Region to take part in the 1948 'Locomotive Exchanges', working on the London Midland Region (St. Pancras-Manchester Central route). The elongated deflectors fitted for the Exchanges remained until May 1957, when work commenced on rebuilding this locomotive, the first of the class to be 'modified'.

'THE ROYAL WESSEX'

'The Royal Wessex' was one of a number of titles introduced by BR from 3rd May 1951 to coincide with the Festival of Britain. Waiting to depart (and for the signals to clear) at Bournemouth Central is 'West Country' Class No. 34108 *Wincanton* with the Up working of this train which, Mondays to Saturdays during 1953, departed here at 8.40am and, calling only at Southampton Central, was scheduled to arrive at Waterloo at 10.50am. The train included portions from Weymouth and (added at Wareham) from Swanage. The main part of the train commenced from Bournemouth West and all portions were brought together at Bournemouth Central. Note another 'light Pacific' partially visible in the bay on the right. *24th June 1953*
No. 34108, the last of the 'West Country' varient of these 'light Pacifics' to be constructed, was only just over three years in traffic and remained in 'as built' condition when photographed here.
The prominent steeple in the background (St. Paul's Church) has long since disappeared; it was damaged in a storm and taken down in 1963. In the 1980s, the remaining part of the church was one of a number of buildings compulsorily purchased and demolished to make way for a major retail development. A replacement church was built a couple of miles to the north.

SOUTHAMPTON CENTRAL – 1

In early-summer 1953, Norman paid a first 'photographic' visit to Southampton. He must have taken a liking to the opportunities offered at Central station, because he was to return here several more times over the following fourteen years. This is just a brief initial foray because, in a few pages hence, we will be back here for more images.

Passing under the impressive gantry of signals at the western (Millbrook) end of the station, No. 34106 *Lydford* restarts the 12.35pm Waterloo-Weymouth. This train also conveyed through carriages for Swanage, detatched at Wareham. Drummond Class 'T9' 4-4-0 No. 30726 waits in the bay, Platform No. 5. *27th June 1953*
As with several other photographers, this became a favourite viewpoint used by Norman. The overbridge towards this end of the station dated from 1934, replacing a level crossing at the east end.

Urie 4-6-0 'King Arthur' Class 'N15' No. 30738 *King Pellinore* waits to depart from Platform 1. This being a Saturday (the summer services having commenced earlier in the month) and with the station clock showing 12.30pm, this must have been the 11.16am Bournemouth West to York and Newcastle. *27th June 1953*
It appears that Norman never made a print from this negative; I suspect he was unhappy with the framing, having 'cut off' the top of the station clock tower. Only approximately half the full width of the original image has been reproduced here.
No. 30738 was the last of the Urie 'King Arthur' 4-6-0s to be withdrawn; from Basingstoke in March 1958 and cut up at Eastleigh. The clock tower, which dated from 1890, was under repair. It had originally suffered damage during the Second World War.

"Where's this one listed in my ABC?" A couple of locospotters watch as diesel electric No. 10000 prepares to depart with the 11.30am Weymouth-Waterloo which, judging from the time displayed by the station clock, was some five minutes down on the scheduled departure time. This train was booked non-stop from Southampton to Waterloo. The train at Platform No. 2, headed by BR Class '4' 2-6-0 No. 76011, was most likely the 10.50am Bristol Temple Meads to Portsmouth Harbour. *27th June 1953*

Diesel electric No. 10000 (and 'twin' No. 10001) had been transferred to the Southern Region (70A) during w/e 7th March 1953. In the event, this proved rather fortuitous because the 'Merchant Navy' Class were soon to be withdrawn, on a temporary basis, following a broken axle incident with No. 35020 Bibby Line whilst passing through Crewkerne at speed on 24th April 1953. Following transfer from the LMR to Nine Elms mpd, the twin English Electric/Ivatt diesels had been allocated to Waterloo-Bournemouth-Weymouth and Waterloo-Exeter top link diagrams.

Four and three-quarters hours later, the same locomotive reappears, now in charge of the Down 'Royal Wessex', the 4.35pm from Waterloo, due at Southampton at 6.08pm. The clock face on the 156ft tower of the Civic Centre shows 6.10pm – that would count as a 'right time' arrival by today's standards! *27th June 1953*

Notice fronting Western Esplanade on the right, part of the once-prominent electricity generating station, which was demolished in 1976.

'King Arthur' Class 'N15' No. 30449 *Sir Torre* sets off from the Down platform with the 12-noon stopping service from Yeovil Junction to Exeter Central. Both main platforms were served by loops off the Up or Down lines and the train featured here is just about to cross back onto the Down main line before commencing the climb towards Honiton Tunnel. *11th October 1955*
Notice, in the right background, the pre-cast concrete face of the sharply curved platform which served the branch line to Seaton. The signal box can be seen beyond and to the right of the single open wagon whilst, to the left, some 6-wheeled tanks await to be refilled at the large milk factory which abutted the Up side of the line.
No. 30449 was the second of a batch of ten of these locomotives officially classified as 'rebuilds' but which were, to all intents and purposes, new engines with tenders reused from Drummond's Class 'G14' dating from 1908. During the BR era, No. 30449 was allocated to Salisbury, from where it was withdrawn in December 1959

SEATON JUNCTION

It appears that Norman made only two visits to Seaton Junction, taking four photographs in 1955 and just a single image in 1964. For the purpose of this book, it makes sense to combine the latter with two from his earlier visit.

No. 30843, one of the final batch of 'S15' Class 4-6-0s to be built, in 1936, recommences its journey with a two-coach local, the 1.55pm from Axminster to Exeter Central. A Class 'M7' 0-4-4T can just be seen at the branch line platform, with a connecting 'pull & push' train, the 2.05pm to Seaton. *11th October 1955*
Despite the leisurely timings allowed for the 1.55pm from Axminster, according to the time Norman logged for this photograph (2.10pm), the train was some eight minutes down on the scheduled departure from Seaton Junction. That might have been the consequence of the preceding through train not keeping to time. The connecting service to Seaton would have been 'held' for the late-running main line stopping train.

Jumping forward some nine years, this proved to be Norman's only photograph to feature Seaton Junction station from the road overbridge, which offered this panoramic view. Rebuilt 'Battle of Britain' Class No. 34082 *615 Squadron* comes thundering past at high speed on the Up through line with a Padstow to Waterloo express, having just descended around 400ft in the five miles from Honiton Tunnel. A Down local waits in the opposite platform. *18th July 1964*

From this camera position, the sharply curved platform at which Seaton Branch trains commenced or completed their journeys was hidden by the side of the cutting in the left foreground. The arms of a pair of signals authorising access from the branch to a siding or the main line can just be seen. Much more prominent are the co-acting Starting signals for the Up through and platform lines. A part of the United Dairies milk depot can be seen beyond the main station building on the Up side.

LYME REGIS BRANCH – A FIRST VISIT

Despite his various forays to the lineside in the vicinity of Honiton Tunnel, Norman did not venture the few miles eastwards to the Lyme Regis Branch until August 1955. Even then, this proved only a brief visit which, probably because he lacked a car, found him proceeding no farther along the branch than the initial mile or so from the main line junction at Axminster.

Two views of Adams radial tank No. 30584 climbing west of Axminster, *en route* to Lyme Regis whilst working Sundays services. The upper view is of the 2.23pm departure, the lower the 4.25pm. The Ayrshire cow seen in the upper view appears quite unfazed by the passage of the train. *7th August 1955 Norman took these photographs of two Sunday afternoon services approximately five and seven minutes after their respective scheduled departure times from Axminster. A few outlying dwellings of that town can be seen in the distance. Nowadays, housing development on the southern side of Axminster has expanded out as far as the route of the former branch line and the A35 dual carriageway cuts across the trackbed at right angles near Abbey Gate.*
We will return to this delightful branch for more comprehensive coverage on reaching the pages featuring the end of the 1950s.

VARIETY AT HONITON TUNNEL

On this occasion, Norman elected to stand closer to the western end of Honiton Tunnel than he usually did when photographing eastbound traffic. No. 35002 *Union Castle* shows a clean exhaust and is very close to completing the stiff climb with the Up 'ACE'. The locomotive looks in remarkably clean external condition, having been released back into traffic the previous month following a visit to works for an overhaul. *6th October 1956*

Maunsell Class 'S15' No. 30826 is in charge of the 12-noon Yeovil Junction to Exeter Central, a stopping service we last featured at Seaton Junction and which called at every station *en route*. Little more than thirty miles and around 65 minutes after departing from Yeovil, the 4-6-0 emerges into weak autumnal sunshine and commences the descent towards Honiton. *6th October 1956*
The summit of the long climbs in both directions coincides with this end of the tunnel, which is dead straight for the full length. Notice that the railway's telegraph wires were routed overland on twin poles, rather than taken through the tunnel.

Another Down local, this time hauled by 'U' Class No. 31794, emerges from the tunnel. *6th October 1956*
This 2-6-0 was one of a small batch which had originally entered service as a SE&CR 'K' ('River') Class 2-6-4T. Built by Armstrong, Whitworth & Company in 1925, the locomotive was numbered A794 and named River Rother. *Conversion to a 2-6-0 was undertaken at Eastleigh in 1928.*

Perhaps, more appropriately, the theme of 'Variety at Honiton Tunnel' should be applied to the traffic rather than the locomotives, as Southern Region main line motive power was by this era dominated by the Bulleid 'Pacifics'. This, the penultimate member of the 'Merchant Navy' Class, No. 35029 *Ellerman Lines*, looks absolutely immaculate and remains much as built by BR, having first entered service in February 1949. She had gained a BR lined green livery in 1952, whilst the small piece of the skirt originally positioned ahead of both outside cylinders had been removed during the same visit to works. Despite the lack of a headboard, Norman logged this train as the Down 'ACE', as can be confirmed by the Nine Elms 'No. 6' engine duty displayed on the lower of the two route discs. *6th October 1956*

'Battle of Britain' Class No. 34053 *Sir Keith Park*, allocated to Salisbury mpd throughout most of the 1950s, heads what Norman recorded as an 'Army Special' over Bridge No. 468. Barely a decade old, this 'light Pacific' was rebuilt in the latter part of 1958. *8th September 1955*

Withdrawn in October 1967, No. 34053 was eventually rebuilt from scrap condition (it was even minus its front bogie and pony truck) by Southern Locomotives Limited. Currently (2015) it can be seen at work on the Severn Valley Railway.

The next member of the class, No. 34054 *Lord Beaverbrook*, was to remain in original form throughout its career, being withdrawn from service in September 1964. It too was based at Salisbury thoughout much of the 1950s. This train was the 10.00am (Sundays) Ilfracombe-Waterloo, which also included through carriages from Bideford added at Barnstaple Junction. *8th September 1957*

EXETER – BLACK BOY TUNNEL

BR Standard Class '3MT' No. 82017 emerges from the eastern portal of Black Boy Tunnel (263 yds) with a service to Exmouth.

This 2-6-2T was one of a batch of the Class '3' 'Standards' built at Swindon and allocated from new to Exmouth Junction. Here, they became regular performers over the Exmouth Branch for a number of years.

More traditionally associated with the Exeter-Exmouth services for many decades were the 'M7' Class 0-4-4Ts. One of a large allocation of these locomotives based at Exmouth Junction, No. 30323 appears to have received at least a partial repaint, together with the later style of BR totem. *Both 27th September 1957*

Notice the concrete post and panel fence bordering the top of the cutting alongside Mount Pleasant Road. These components had been cast at the nearby (almost adjoining) SR Concrete Works sited on the Up side of the line here at Exmouth Junction.

Rebuilt only six months earlier, immaculately groomed No. 35009 *Shaw Savill* **bursts out of the tunnel and approaches Exmouth Junction with the Up 'ACE'.** *27th September 1957*
The footpath, descending on the right of this and the views opposite, had provided access to the Up platform of Mount Pleasant Road Halt which, as an early casualty of local bus services, was closed on 2nd January 1928.

Climbing the 1 in 100 gradient away from Exeter Central, No. 35003 *Royal Mail* approaches St. James' Park Halt with the 8.15am Plymouth (Friary)–Waterloo express. *15th April 1957 No. 35022 had taken over this train at Exeter (Exmouth Junction Duty No. 496). Another Exmouth Junction locomotive (working Duty No. 539 and usually allocated to a 'West Country' Class) will have brought the train from Plymouth to Exeter.*

No. 35029 *Ellerman Lines* **completes her 171¾ mile run from Waterloo with the Down 'ACE'. Calls were made at Salisbury (water taken and the rear carriage taken off and attached to a stopping train serving intermediate stations west of Salisbury) and Sidmouth Junction (where further carriages were taken off to serve Sidmouth and Exmouth). Here at Exeter Central, the train would be further divided, with portions for Ilfracombe, Torrington, Bude, Padstow and Plymouth.** *27th September 1957*
Note the asbestos cement clad carriage stock shed on the Down side. This was built on the site of the original locomotive shed after much larger facilities had been provided at Exmouth Junction.

EXETER STATIONS

A visit to St. Davids at 8.45am on a Saturday morning witnessed Class 'T9' 4-4-0 No. 30710 and Class 'N' 2-6-0 No. 31842 entering Platform 2 with what Norman recorded as an excursion to Windsor. *28th September 1957*
It appears that Norman never bothered to make a print, possibly because the development of the plate was faulty and by reason that the nearside platform canopy cast a shadow along the sides of both locomotives and the leading carriages of the train. However, it represents only one of two photographs Norman took featuring Southern Region Steam at Exeter St. Davids, and thanks to the digital imaging skills of our publisher, it is (just about!) worthy of inclusion.

ROMSEY

Class 'M7' 0-4-4T No. 30028 slows to call at Romsey with a local service from Eastleigh to Andover Junction, a journey which was scheduled to occupy just two minutes short of an hour. *24th September 1958*
The line from Eastleigh lies out of sight behind the train. The line seen curving away sharply to the right is the later route which follows the lower Test Valley towards Redbridge, where the Southampton-Bournemouth main line is joined.

SOUTHAMPTON CENTRAL – 2

'West Country' No. 34019 *Bideford* is ready to restart the 11.00am Bournemouth West to Waterloo away from a scheduled three-minute call at No. 1 platform. Booked departure was 12.15pm so, according to the station clock, the train was running to time. *26th September 1958*
A Nine Elms allocation since April 1951, No. 34019 would transfer to Brighton less than a month after having been photographed here by Norman. Notice, this time, he succeeded in framing the image to incorporate the full height of the clock tower, including the weather vane.

'Schools' Class 4-4-0 No. 30936 *Cranleigh* approaches Platform 4 with the 11.00am Brighton-Cardiff cross country service, which included a portion from Portsmouth Harbour added to the through train at Fareham. *24th September 1958*

Dominating the skyline in this direction, the 156ft high tower of the Civic Centre, a part of the West Wing completed in November 1933. Other than the distinctive western portal to the railway tunnel, it's about the only structure still identifiable nowadays from this same viewpoint. Note the 'level crossing' road sign. Coal supplied to the electricity generating station on the opposite side of the road was delivered via a siding until this was taken out of use at the start of the 1950s. The Morris Minor is crossing the rails which remained set into the road surface until late-1963.

BR Class '3' 2-6-2T No. 82015 (built at Swindon in 1951) approaches No. 3 Platform with a local service. Judging from the time showing on the Civic Centre clock, this was most likely the 4.18pm Eastleigh-Totton, which was scheduled to arrive at Southampton at 4.28pm. *25th September 1958*
The two leading coaches are formed of one of only two articulated sets ever used by the Southern Railway. The pair seen here must have been Set 514, the other, Set 513, having been withdrawn the previous November. They were conversions of former SE&CR railmotors and had been used on the Sheppey Light Railway until this closed in 1950. Thereafter, both sets endured a rather nomadic existence. Never, as sometimes claimed, fitted for 'Pull & Push' working, this set was withdrawn in October 1959.

A busy scene back at the western end of the station finds 'West Country' No. 34097 *Holsworthy*, having only recently been transferred to Brighton, setting off with the 11.30am Brighton-Plymouth. No. 30862 *Lord Collingwood* takes on water at Platform 4 before resuming a westbound journey with Eastleigh duty No. 252, the 11.30m Waterloo to Bournemouth West. *23rd April 1959*
No. 34097 is oft-quoted as having been transferred to Brighton (from Bournemouth) in March 1959 yet here, a month later, the locomotive still carries a 71B shed plate but the service worked was Brighton Duty No. 732, so perhaps it is more the case that the shed plate was yet to be changed. She was rebuilt early in 1961, having run in the form seen here for only a little over eleven years. A mere five years later, No. 34097 was withdrawn and sold for scrap.

CANUTE ROAD CROSSING

Two flagmen halt traffic on Canute Road to enable 'U' Class 2-6-0 No. 31803 to pull out from the Eastern Docks with an Ocean Liner baggage train. Although it is barely visible in his left hand, the flagman to the left is also holding (and doubtless using) a bell. *25th September 1958*

Notice the distinctive brick and stone gate pillars, the right-hand pier mostly obscured by the locomotive. These piers and the two buildings seen to the right still exist in 2015. The nearer, single-storey structure, erected in 1907, was the former 'Wilts & Dorset Bank' but here mostly occupied by the Western Union. The larger building, known as 'Pilgrim House', was originally a Mercantile Marine Office dating from the 1880s, which was later occupied by the Department of Trade & Industry. It is now a Chinese restaurant and takeaway. The other motive power includes, to the left, a Standard Vanguard (Phase 1A) car built between late-1951 and March 1953. It carries a London registration. To the right is a 3-wheeled Heinkel Kabine 'Bubblecar', one of a number of designs which proved popular as an economical form of transport during the 1950s and early '60s. Many still exist but their popularity was eclipsed by the introduction of the British Austin and Morris 'Minis' in 1959.

SOUTHAMPTON TUNNEL

'West Country' No. 34093 *Saunton* emerges from the eastern end of Southampton Tunnel and makes for Tunnel Junction with the 11.00am Bournemouth–Waterloo service. A Nine Elms shedplate (70A) had been carried since the previous year, when this 4-6-2 was reallocated from Bournemouth. *23rd April 1959*

This was a 'one-off' visit; just two photographs were taken at this location, and 'that was it' as far as Norman was concerned! He must have been standing on the steps of a footbridge passing over the railway and linking New Road to North Front. The latter features in the left foreground (note the solitary moped), as do some flats (being part of 'Kingsland House') immediately beyond. A lineside location seemingly neglected by most railway photographers, the substantial growth of foliage over the past several decades makes this 'open' view extending across Palmerston Park all but impossible to replicate nowadays.

SALISBURY, TUNNEL JUNCTION – SUNSHINE AND SHADOWS

From one tunnel to another; this example is at Salisbury. Standing in the fork of the junction, with his back to the signal box, Norman was able to see through all 443 yards of Fisherton Tunnel. Class 'N15' 4-6-0 No. 30453 *King Arthur* emerges to take the main line and bear left around a curve subject to a permanent speed restriction, with the 12.58pm stopping train from Salisbury to Waterloo. *29th September 1959*

No. 35016 *Elders Fyffes* drifts around the sharp curve past Salisbury Tunnel Junction signal box with the Down 'Atlantic Coast Express' and crosses the junction with the original route to Romsey, Eastleigh and Southampton. *29th September 1959*
The signal box was taken out of use in 1981. Note the pair of railway cottages with the sloping pathway leading from the garden gate down to the box. A Wilts & Dorset double-decker bus passes over London Road Bridge (No. 228) on the A30 Andover to Salisbury road.

SALISBURY

'Merchant Navy' No. 35017 *Belgian Marine* arrives with the 3.0pm Waterloo-Plymouth, which also conveyed through carriages to Ilfracombe and Torrington. A connecting service, the 4.54pm all stations to Templecombe, can be seen waiting in the adjacent bay platform (No. 5). *23rd April 1959*

Norman took several fine photographs at Salisbury station. Most have been published before, including this example taken towards the west end of Platforms 4 (left) and 5. However, when first published, the image was taken from a print, made by Norman, which omitted everything to the right of the 'Salisbury' nameboard on the end of the platform canopy. In so doing, he cropped from this scene the connecting train, so this scan shows the entire plate. Perhaps Norman decided to exclude what, in the steam era, had been a regular sight at Salisbury – the use of a motorised water bowser to replenish the tanks for the carriage toilets. All these years later, it is exactly the kind of detail which makes these photographs more interesting. Notice also the porter pushing a 2-wheeled sack truck with a very full load of mail bags.

At the opposite end of the station, 'King Arthur' Class 'N15' No. 30448 *Sir Tristram* sets off from Platform 2, to pass around the severe curve with a train bound for Waterloo. *1st October 1959*
The bay platform (No. 6), on the left, leads to Platform 4, used for through Southern Region traffic. Platform 3 was used primarily for traffic bound for the former GWR cross-country route via Westbury. Platform 1 (here unseen) accommodated traffic from the Western Region. Today, only the latter platform is out of use for passenger trains. The low-pitched roof of the former GWR terminus can seen to the right of No. 30448 but is mostly obscured by a nearer flat-roofed structure.

Just a single image here (but we return later) showing a variety of motive power lined up outside part of the large depot (at this time coded 72B), situated on the south side of the main line about a half-mile west of the station. On parade, from left to right, are BR 'Standard' Class '5' 4-6-0 No. 73114, 'U' Class 2-6-0 No. 31614, 'T9' 4-4-0 No. 30301 and a BR Class '4' 4-6-0. *23rd March 1958*

Class 'M7' 0-4-4T No. 30104, about a mile east of Poole station, at the Parkstone end of an embankment which separated the large boating lake in Poole Park from the waters of Poole Harbour. The train was the 11.28am Brokenhurst-Bournemouth Central which – following the original route of the Southampton & Dorchester Railway – ran via Ringwood and Broadstone, a distance of about 32 miles as against the later direct route of just 7¾ miles. *3rd October 1959*
The bridge in the foreground crosses Whitecliff Road and the locality is still known locally as 'The Bunny' (this being the name adopted for the nearby sluice, which enables the levels of the lake, opened in 1890, to be regulated via a culvert passing under the railway embankment). Milepost 112¾ is prominent by the lineside in the foreground.

'THE BUNNY'

'West Country' Class No. 34041 *Wilton*, in charge of a Weymouth-Waterloo train, is about to get to grips with the 1 in 60/50 grades of Parkstone Bank, doubtless having gained as much speed as possible in the mile since setting off from the call at Poole. *3rd October 1959*
This was a member of the class which never received a 'civic shield', usually affixed under the nameplates on both sides of the 'air-smoothed' cladding.
It is several decades since the waters of Parkstone Bay lapped against this railway embankment, following a reclamation scheme that created a ribbon of land which now forms Harbourside Park. A corner of Poole boating lake can just be seen through the trees to the right in both views.

PARKSTONE BANK

Returning briefly to an earlier period in the 1950s, Norman took up position just to the east of Parkstone station (located immediately beyond the overbridge seen in the background) to take several photographs of trains climbing the incline towards the summit near Branksome. Veteran Drummond Class 'T9' No. 30283 was in charge of the 9.25am Salisbury to Bournemouth West, a service via the 'Salisbury & Dorset Junction' line, which called at every station *en route*. *24th June 1953*

EAST OF AXMINSTER

We are back on the SR West of England main line; *'East of Axminster'* was all that Norman recorded to remind him of the location. 'Merchant Navy' No. 35003 *Royal Mail* attacks the easier adverse grades, running ahead of a storm, with the 8.26am Plymouth to Waterloo. *30th March 1959*

Having first examined a print which Norman made of this image, there was little other than the overbridge to provide any clue as to the exact location. But when emailed a scan of the complete glass plate, this revealed Ivo Peters' Bentley and a track climbing towards the overbridge, both seen to the left (Down) side of the railway (Norman had decided to exclude this part of the negative when making the print). So, it did not take too much detective work to establish that this is Fosse Way Bridge, which carries the A358 obliquely across the main line just under a couple of miles east of Axminster station, on the section between Axe Gates and Broom Gates level crossings.

OPPOSITE PAGE TOP: This full side-view of No. 30584 was taken at Exmouth Junction motive power depot, situated on the north-eastern side of Exeter. All three remaining examples of these radial tanks were based here for use on the Lyme Regis Branch. The other locomotive just poking into view was 'Z' Class No. 30953, one of the impressive 0-8-0Ts whose duties included banking trains up the severe gradient between Exeter St. Davids and Central stations.
Each week, one of the trio of radial tanks was returned from Lyme Regis (where there was a small one-road locomotive shed) to Exmouth Junction, for the boiler to be washed out and to receive any necessary maintenance. No. 30584, built by Dübs & Co. in 1885 (but subsequently modified and last reboilered in 1948), would return to branch line duties the following Saturday and another of the trio would be brought across to Exmouth Junction for similar attention.

OPPOSITE PAGE BOTTOM: We had best start at Axminster with this image of No. 30583, it being the only example of these radial tanks destined to survive. On withdrawal it was purchased by the Bluebell Railway, where it was in steam until 1990 but since then has been on display as a static exhibit whilst awaiting an extensive overhaul. These elderly locomotives, the challenging 1 in 40 gradients and severe curvature encountered on this branch line, coupled with the delightful and remote countryside through which it passed, provided the combination of factors which so appealed to both photographers. This 'old lady' – already seventy-four years had passed since she was built by Neilson & Co. in 1885 – sets off (3 minutes late according to the time logged by Norman) with the 5.42pm (Sundays) service to Lyme Regis, from the bay platform sited on the Up side of the main line. *23rd August 1959*
The lined black livery had been applied when No. 30583 was overhauled (which had included a replacement boiler) and repainted at the start of 1959; this including the 'modernised' style of BR crest first introduced a couple of years earlier. The two coaches comprised (front) a red-liveried former SE&CR non-corridor example and (rear) an SR Maunsell-designed Corridor Brake Composite (BCK). Note, in the left background, the tall water tower whilst, to the right, the cattle pens, a once-familiar feature at many a market town or country station. The low level sign at the side of the far end of the loop line warned of 'Trap Points'.

SECTION 4
THE EARLY 1960s
THE LYME REGIS BRANCH

Norman Lockett and Ivo Peters visited this delightful 6¾ mile branch on a number of occasions, and the photographs taken in 1959 and '60 must surely rank amongst the finest of the many in monochrome that have been published featuring this line. Judge for yourselves because we have deliberately brought together a sizeable number of images dating from the end of the 1950s into the start of the 'Swinging Sixties'. Ivo also took photographs during these visits but concentrated more on filming scenes in 16mm colour. Norman even resorted to some 35mm colour transparencies! Some of the images which follow have been published before (nearly twenty-five years ago) but they were reproduced from Norman's prints.

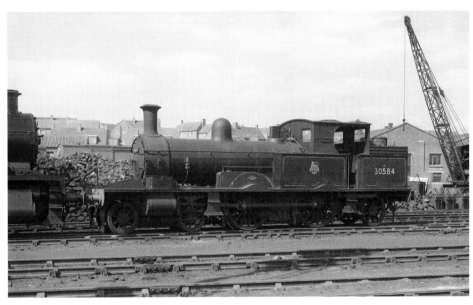

About a couple of miles out from Axminster, No. 30584 emits a fierce exhaust on the 1 in 40 climb south of Wyke Green, having just passed around a curve which brought the track through a ninety degree change of direction to the west of Trinity Hill. In the background, the line can be seen emerging from the cutting to the far left, the route marked by a row of white concrete fencing posts and a telegraph pole. *18th April 1960*
Note the difference between the front ends of the frames of No's 30583 and 30584 as seen in these various images; the former still retained the curved profile of the original design. Since the previous year (1959), when No. 30583 had been repainted, both locomotives could be identified much more easily from a distance by the BR crests applied on the sides of the tanks, No. 30584 still displaying the early BR 'Lion & Wheel' design from when repainted in 1951.

Other than the summer season, a single coach usually sufficed for the normal branch line traffic. No. 30583 here looks a little travel weary but nothing that some oily rags and lots of elbow grease would not solve. As seen in these images, more often the paintwork of all three of the radial tanks was maintained in a 'well-polished' condition. *27th December 1960*
Norman generally ceased his photography each year towards the end of October and recommenced the following spring. He developed the glass plate negatives within a week or so of taking individual photographs. However, he left the printing and enlarging, of those he deemed worthy, until the winter months. So a photograph taken during late December was an exception. But, in 1960, Christmas Day fell on the Sunday, so Tuesday 27th counted as a Bank Holiday and, it appears, here is how Norman decided to spend the day.

No. 30584 climbs through an attractive wooded section of the line just to the east of Bulmoor Cross; the trees – other than the Willow to the left – yet to break into leaf. *18th April 1960*

Note, in a number of these photographs taken during 1960, there are signs of rails waiting to be replaced. During the early part of that year, much of the track along the branch was renewed as part of a programme to upgrade the line for the use of LMR Ivatt Class '2' 2-6-2Ts, the arrival of which would herald the demise of the elderly radial tanks in 1961; albeit – as mentioned earlier – that one would be purchased for restoration and use by the Bluebell Railway.

Following an all-too-brief level 'breather' from the hard climbing, No. 30583 is bound for Lyme and going well, the sunshine reflecting off the 4-4-2T's bright, clean paintwork. *6th June 1960*
There were three stretches of 1 in 40 adverse gradient between Axminster and Combpyne. This is the start of the last section, following which the gradients eased. There was even a short section of downgrade, as the line swung around the western flank of Shapwick Hill, before climbing was resumed towards the summit of the line just beyond Combpyne station. Note yet more evidence of impending track renewal.

With a load which included the addition of a through coach from Waterloo, No. 30584 had stalled on the 1 in 40 climb towards Hartgrove Farm. A quick check revealed the smokebox door was not fully secured, so the problem was soon overcome. All of this was witnessed by Norman and here's Ivo, having filmed and photographed the event, watching No. 30584 getting slowly into her stride again and, now somewhat behind the scheduled time, heading off towards Combpyne. *6th June 1960*
Note the gradient post to the near side of No. 30584. It was the only one on the branch which indicated a rising gradient in both directions (so it has proved easy to work out the location, using a gradient profile of the line and an OS map!).

No. 30583 pulls away from Combpyne, the only intermediate station on the line and comprising just a single platform. The train is bound for Lyme Regis and the summit of the line is reached, 500ft above sea level, just a few yards further into this cutting. *6th June 1960*

The platform was devoid of any buildings. These were positioned closer to the lane leading to the village, which lies almost three-quarters of a mile to the west. In earlier years there was a loop and Combpyne was fully signalled. Post-war, for nearly two decades, there was a Camping Coach provided here for the summer months. Hidden by the departing train in this view, it was stabled at the end of the siding occupied here by the SR Utility Van.

The other representative of the three Adams radial tanks retained for use on this line, No. 30582, crosses Cannington Viaduct with a Lyme Regis-Axminster service. The route of the line here ran parallel with the coast – just a mile to the south – before, in the Up direction, swinging away northwards to the summit and Combpyne station. *30th March 1959*

You will notice from the date of this and the following few images, that we've slipped back into 1959 in order to keep these photographs of this branch line together. The 10-arch Cannington Viaduct, the only major engineering feature on this line, is seen as viewed from the south. Built in concrete and completed in 1903 (following which the line was opened on 24th August that year), it is 203yds long. During construction, considerable problems were encountered in stabilising the structure from settlement, especially at the western end. The works to arrest such movement included building a secondary 'Jack Arch' into the third span from the Combpyne end. Note the 'hump' created by the settlement, as revealed by the parapet falling 'out of level' towards the west (left) end. The structure survives and has been Grade II listed since 1986.

'The biter bit(ten)'. Both Ivo and his Bentley (NHY 581) feature in this scene at Shapwick Green as No. 30582, with coaches comprising a pair of Maunsell Corridor Composite Brakes, descends the 1 in 40 leading towards Cannington Viaduct ... whilst (INSET RIGHT) here is the photograph taken by Ivo (*courtesy of Julian Peters*), *30th March 1959*
Given the '*Law of Averages*', you are much more likely to spot Norman appearing somewhere in a photograph taken by Ivo, as against the other way around; a consequence of their differing 'styles', Norman generally (but – as seen here – by no means always) choosing a position closer to the lineside than that usually adopted by Ivo.

No. 30582 drifts around the sweeping reverse curves near Uplyme, about a mile before the terminus at Lyme Regis (to reach which the train will cross the county boundary from Devon into Dorset).
30th March 1959

This scene was captured from the overbridge which carried Gore Lane across the railway. The pair of distinctive houses in the left background are to be found in Cuckoo Lane but when the writer visited the same location just a few years ago, this view from the bridge had become totally obscured by the trees and vegetation which have self-seeded and grown since the branch line closed in late-November 1965. Cannington Viaduct lies about a half mile beyond and to the left of the point where the line disappears from this view into a cutting. This is as close as Norman got to photographing the terminus. Either he was not sufficiently impressed by the single platform station, perched some 250ft above sea level, to expend even one negative or, more likely, had already used all the glass plates he carried that day.

DOUBLE-HEADED DELIGHT

To round off scenes from the Lyme Regis Branch, the following three photographs are included as examples of what was undoubtably the added attraction that drew Norman (usually with Ivo Peters) to the line on a summer Saturday or – as was the case here – on certain Bank Holidays; namely the through workings of coaches to and from Waterloo. These coaches were detached from a main line train at Axminster, then added to the branch line train and taken forward to Lyme Regis. The additional weight, over such a heavily graded line, required two of the radial tanks working in tandem. A reverse procedure occured with London-bound through coaches from the seaside terminus.

Over the years, the trains and timings tended to vary from summer to summer and on some of the Bank Holidays. Taking 1959 as an example, the Summer Saturdays Only through workings were as follows:

Down branch line services from Axminster – the 11.35am to Lyme Regis conveyed through coaches off the 8.05am ex-Waterloo and, similarly, the 1.50pm branch line departure included the rear portion of the 10.45am ex-Waterloo

In the Up line direction – through coaches off the 9.00am and 3.05pm departures from Lyme Regis were added at Axminster to the 8.30am Exeter Central-Waterloo and the 12.45pm Torrington-Waterloo.

Maximum effort on nearing the top of a gruelling stretch at 1 in 40, having just passed under the road bridge near Hartgrove Farm. This was the 4.36pm from Axminster, which conveyed through coaches from Waterloo and required the combined efforts of both No's 30584 and 30583. It was a beautiful sunny day but quite a fresh wind, with the train hereabouts having climbed to around 475ft above sea level. *6th June 1960*
Norman and Ivo (the latter filmed this and several other of the trains as photographed by Norman*) must have heard this pair of 'veterans' approaching for several minutes before finally appearing into view. Little wonder this branch line, in the late 1950s and early '60s, had become a favourite haunt of several other well-known railway photographers.
The day of this visit was Whit Monday 1960 and – for those perhaps too young to remember – this was a Bank Holiday, the date of which fluctuated from year to year. In 1978, it was replaced by the fixed date Spring (late May) Bank Holiday

* See the DVD *Ivo Peters – His films revisited: Steam in 1960.*

No's 30584 and 30583 appear around the bend heading for Lyme Regis with a service which conveyed through coaches from Waterloo. *6th June 1960*
Norman only rarely resorted to 'low level' shots as seen on this page – a 'worm's eye view', to coin the phrase Ivo always used!

Later in the day and with the evening shadows already beginning to lengthen, the same pair of locomotives pass through the wooded section *en route* for Lyme Regis. *6th June 1960*
Again, Ivo was filming and photographing the same train, from a field above the line to the left. It was, he recalled to me many years ago, the end of a most enjoyable and memorable day; sentiments which are echoed by these iconic images captured by Norman.

THE 'GREYHOUND' RAILTOUR

This railtour, organised by the Railway Correspondence & Travel Society (RCTS), ran from Waterloo to Salisbury, where Class 'T9' 4-4-0 No. 30718 took over. The immaculate Drummond 'Greyhound' continued with the Special to Yeovil Junction, then – following a reversal and via South Junction – to Yeovil Pen Mill. There, a second reversal was needed in order to proceed towards Weymouth. Norman photographed the train near Clifton Maybank, just south of Yeovil, shortly after it had passed under the Salisbury-Exeter main line. *14th August 1960*

'The South Western Ltd', 1960

Another railtour, 'The South Western Limited', organised by the 'Locomotive Club of Great Britain' (LCGB), set forth from London, Cannon Street, for a brief visit to Eastleigh Works. From Eastleigh, Urie Class 'H16' 4-6-2T No. 30516 took over and is here passing through Southampton Central. To the right, a 'Merchant Navy' Class (thought to be No. 35016 *Elders Fyffes*) is about to proceed with the Down 'Bournemouth Belle', which unlike the Special has been given 'two pegs' on the signal gantry. *18th September 1960*

A pair of these heavy 4-6-2Ts had been allocated to Eastleigh to work oil trains to Fawley, which was the destination of this next leg of the LCGB Special. Unfortunately, not ideal lighting for taking this photograph with the resultant image a little dark but it represents a rare opportunity to feature an 'H16'.

At Totton, Class 'N15' 4-6-0 No. 30782 *Sir Brian* waits for the railtour to return from the branch line to Fawley. *18th September 1960*
The 'King Arthur' was beautifully presented and would take the tour forward to Wimborne and Broadstone, where S&D Class '7F' No. 53804 came onto the train to proceed to Templecombe, then (a real treat for the enthusiasts) up the main line to Salisbury. Peter Mumford's Flour Mill, the prominant building seen behind the tender of the 4-6-0, was still rail-served at this date although the single siding appears to have witnessed little trade of late. The mill has since been converted to offices. Unfortunately, Norman's camera position resulted in a pole apparently emerging from the chimney of the locomotive and a vent pipe from the steam dome (it sometimes happened even to the most experienced of railway photographers!).

Whilst Norman waited at Totton for the special to arrive from Fawley, 'West Country' Class No. 34108 *Wincanton* came speeding past with a Waterloo to Weymouth express.
18th September 1960
The line seen curving away to the right of the signal gantry in the background, located at the western end of Totton station Down platform, was the freight only Eling Branch. This served various industrial premises and wharfage to which sea-going vessels gained access via the River Test estuary.

'THE SOLENT LIMITED'

Ths was a railtour organised by the Locomotive Club of Great Britain, which commenced at Waterloo and, initially, ran to Portsmouth Harbour. From there, Drummond Class 'T9' 4-4-0 No. 30117 took control of the Special for the next leg to Fareham.

From Fareham station, the Special was taken along the southern end of the former Meon Valley line as far as Droxford (by then the current railhead). This line had once served as part of the through route to Gosport (and Stokes Bay), which was the next point of call for the railtour. For these legs of the tour, the train was hauled by Class 'E1' 0-6-0T No. 32694 and Class 'O2' 0-4-4T No. 30200. Here they depart Gosport, which had been closed to passenger traffic since early June 1953, although freight continued to be handled until early 1969.

This must have been one of the last duties of No. 32694, then the sole remaining example of this class, as she was withdrawn just three months later. That might explain the lack of a shedplate.

Arrival back at Fareham, with No. 30117 waiting to take over for the next leg to Southampton where, behind other motive power, the Special made a visit to the docks. Then followed a call into Eastleigh Works, before heading back to London via the Midland & South Western Junction route as far as Newbury; thence to Reading to regain 'Southern' rails back to Waterloo.

No. 30117 was withdrawn in July 1961. No. 30200 survived into the following year.

AN 'M7' ON THE SWANAGE BRANCH

The following three images (below and overleaf), featuring Swanage-Wareham branch line services, were all taken during the afternoon of Sunday 23rd July 1961. Bournemouth-allocated Class 'M7' 0-4-4T No. 30328 was working the branch. However, if the writer has done his research correctly, this member of the class was not a long-term performer on this line.

Unfortunately, I don't have access to a *Summer 1962 Time Table* but judging from the times that Norman noted for each photograph, the schedule for Sunday afternoons in 1962 must have remained the same or very similar to that in the *Summer 1957 Time Table*.

No. 30328 is seen climbing away from the outskirts of Swanage and passing under Washpond Lane Bridge; the time was 2.35pm. A ten-compartment strengthening coach, of South Eastern & Chatham Railway origin and generally berthed at Swanage for such use, had been added to the usual Maunsell pull-push set.
To the far side of this bridge is the present day Herston Halt, constructed by the Swanage Railway and served by steam trains since 1986, the rails having been relaid this far from Swanage in 1984.

Norman next photographed the same 0-4-4T some ninety minutes later, whilst it was working the service from Swanage following that featured in the first photograph. In this scene, the train had just passed under the main Corfe to Swanage road (A351).

Finally, and now north-west of Corfe Castle, No. 30328 climbs towards Norden, passing the 'Whistle' board for a crossing used by lorries. These collected ball clay at a loading point served by the nearby narrow gauge system. The time was 5.42pm.
The prominent feature in the background is East Hill, from the top of which panoramic views may be obtained, including that of the delightfully restored station at Corfe Castle, which much resembles a model railway when seen from such an elevated position.

Another member of the same class, No. 30379 climbs away from Corfe Castle and has just passed over the three-arched viaduct. With the 1962 summer season now ended, just the usual two-coach 'Pull & Push' set was more than sufficient to accommodate passenger numbers. *24th September 1962*

This study, taken during a different visit, shows 'M7' Class 0-4-4T No. 30060 with a Sunday afternoon train from Swanage to Wareham, having just passed under Holme Lane, about a mile short of reaching the main line at Worgret Junction, west of Wareham station. *7th May 1961*

Despite its tidy external appearance, No. 30060 was withdrawn from Bournemouth mpd just two months later. Soon, it is likley that the sight and sound of one of these fine old locomotives will again be seen and heard passing along this section of the line. Following a £1.47 million Coastal Communities Grant awarded in February 2013, in support of 'Project Wareham', the Swanage Railway hopes their first DMU's will start running a Community Rail Service linking Wareham and Swanage (initially on a two year trial basis, projected to commence in the spring of 2016). In the longer term there is a possibility that steam might operate such services on an occasional or special events basis. This could include use of the Swanage Railway's restored Class 'M7' No. 30053 hauling heritage coaching stock but only if the costs to bring and maintain this motive power and stock to a certified main line running standard can be justified. Judging by everything the Swanage Railway has achieved to date, all such hurdles will be overcome.

ISLE OF WIGHT - 1

At the end of May 1961, Norman and Ivo set sail for a visit to the Isle of Wight. They concentrated their photography along a specific section of the line. After a few shots taken at both ends of Ryde Pier, they settled on the busy section between Ryde St. Johns Road and Smallbrook Junction. The latter place was to their liking, being reasonably remote and out in the countryside. As the *Summer Time Table* had already or was about to come into force, this length of the line was being worked as a double track block section. At other times of the year, it reverted to two parallel single

lines from St. Johns Road, when – with the diminutive signal box at Smallbrook Junction taken out of use – one section extended the 3½ miles to Brading on the Ventnor line, and the other 4¼ miles to Haven Street on the Newport and Cowes line.

By the time of this first visit, the motive power comprised a fleet of nineteen ex-L&SWR Class 'O2' 0-4-4Ts (four more had been withdrawn in the mid-1950s). The last two examples of the 'E1' 0-6-0Ts allocated to the Isle of Wight system (No's W3 and W4) had been withdrawn in 1959 and 1960.

Ryde Pier Head station on a rather overcast day. No. W35 *Freshwater* **prepares to depart from Platform 2 with a mid-afternoon train for Cowes.** *2nd June 1961*
Effectively there were three parallel pier structures: the Promenade Pier from which Norman took this photograph; the Tramway Pier, used to support the pair of tracks seen in the foreground, dating from 1864 (and along which tram cars shuttled to and fro until closure in late-January 1969); and the Railway Pier, which was brought into use in 1880. Only one of the platform faces now remains in use for the former London underground train stock which provides the present-day services between Ryde Pier Head and Shanklin.

OPPOSITE PAGE TOP: No. W20 *Shanklin* **arrives at Ryde Esplanade station with a Ventnor line service, having completed the run along the pier.** *2nd June 1961*
The dome of the pier pavilion, opened in 1895 and demolished in 1971, is visible in the distance as is the Pier Head signal box. The latter controlled the release, by Annett's Key, of the crossover seen linking the two running lines and which was retained for emergency use. Only this nearside platform now remains in use.

OPPOSITE PAGE BOTTOM: At the southern end of the platforms, No. W30 *Shorwell* **sets off around the curve with another train bound for the Ventnor line.**
31st May 1961
From here, the line descends at 1 in 50 to pass through Ryde Tunnel and reach the town's third station at St. John's Road. This section of the line from the Pier Head to St. Johns Road had been built jointly for the L&SWR and LB&SCR. To the extreme right, the land here became part of the Hovercraft Terminal.

No. W32 *Bonchurch* pulls away from Ryde St. Johns Road. Located 1½ miles from Pier Head, this was the location of both Ryde mpd and the island's railway works, a corner of which can be seen to the extreme right in this view. *2nd June 1961*
Only two of the four dolls on the signal gantry carry an arm, this confirming the lines towards Smallbrook were being worked as a normal double track block section. The locomotive depot was situated to the rear of the signal box, the coaling stage and approach sidings being seen to the left.

No. W24 *Calbourne* gathers speed as it heads away from Ryde St. Johns Road with a Ventnor train that has been strengthened to a six-coach formation. *2nd June 1961*
Note one of the route discs, instead of being removed, has been turned through 180 degrees.

At the same location as seen opposite, this is Norman's only photograph of a non-passenger train in action on the island (so worthy of this full page image). No. W16 *Ventnor* heads southwards with a short train of coal. A part of Ryde town forms the backdrop. *2nd June 1961*

The writer is no expert on the operation of traffic on the island, so clarification will be welcomed as to why (what appears to be) a coal train is heading in this direction. All coal for the island – domestic, industrial and railway use – was landed at Medina Wharf, on the Newport-Cowes line. For most of the railway's life, coal traffic to Ventnor would most likely have run via Newport, Merstone and Sandown. However, the Merstone-Sandown route closed in February 1956. Thereafter, I'm surmising trains such as that shown here would have run from Newport, via Smallbrook Junction, to Ryde St. Johns Road, where the locomotive could run round. The train could then head south towards Ventnor. Why, otherwise, would this train be heading south from Ryde?

A little farther away from Ryde, Norman took this photograph from the overbridge at Smallbrook Lane. No. W30 *Shorwell* heads around the curve towards Smallbrook Junction with a late-afternoon service to Ventnor. *31st May 1961*

At Smallbrook Junction (the signal box is sited just behind the camera position), it's No. W30 *Shorwell* that features again, here passing onto the line towards Ashey with a train bound for Newport and Cowes. The fireman prepares to collect the single line token from the signalman, which will be carried through to Haven Street. *2nd June 1961*
The rather isolated location of this junction will be apparent, a factor that would have appealed to Norman and Ivo.

The final scene on this visit to the island is the only one taken beyond Smallbrook Junction and then only by a short distance. No. W35 *Freshwater* heads towards Brading with a Ventnor line service. *2nd June 1961*
Norman logged no details of the location other than 'near Smallbrook Junction'. However, based on the time which elapsed between taking this and the previous photographs, the guess is that Smallbrook Junction lies around the curve to the rear of the train, in which case the wooded area on the left is (according to the OS map) Swanpond Copse.

UNUSUAL VISITORS

Norman did not reveal in his notes whether he had prior knowledge or just stumbled across this very unusual visitor to Salisbury motive power depot in September 1962. Beattie well tank 2-4-0 No. 30587 was one of the trio of these famous elderly locomotives which had only recently been displaced from their duties, based at Wadebridge for the Wenford Bridge Branch, by a trio of ex-GWR '1366' Class pannier tanks. Apparently No. 30587 had called in at Salisbury mpd to be watered and coaled during what must have been one of several essential interruptions to a time consuming journey all the way from Wadebridge to her destination at Eastleigh Works.

Pending departure for Eastleigh, No. 30587 was placed alongside BR Class '9F' 2-10-0 No. 92231; a more unlikely combination would be hard to imagine, with the well tank (then) eighty-eight years since having first been placed into service, and the 'Nine' a mere four years! *29th September 1962*
Norman had last photographed one of these little locomotives during a brief visit to Wadebridge in the summer of 1934. By 1962, the trio of well tanks still to be found at Wadebridge, No's 30585/6/7, were by far the most elderly locomotives at work on BR. No. 30587, officially withdrawn in December 1962, was selected for preservation. Today, she forms a part of the collection held by the National Railway Museum but, since restored to working order, has visited several of the various preserved railways in this country. No. 30585 has also survived and is based (2015) at the Buckinghamshire Railway Centre.

The Home Counties Railway Club organised a special from Paddington to Swindon and back hauled by Maunsell No. 30850 *Lord Nelson*. Having arrived on the Down Main running line (nearest the camera and adjacent to Rodbourne Lane Signal Box), the 4-6-0 reversed the train onto the Up Main then, as witnessed here, ran forward onto a siding from which the passengers could alight to visit Swindon Works. No. 30850 was withdrawn two months later (although, of course, is still in existence). *24th June 1962*
The itinerary at Swindon also included visits to the mpd and the newly opened GW Railway Museum, a converted chapel in Faringdon Road. This was the predecessor to STEAM, the present Museum of the Great Western Railway, which is located within part of the former works complex.

A busy scene at Sidmouth Junction as Basingstoke-based 'Schools' Class 4-4-0 No. 30925 *Cheltenham* sets off with an Up train. Running light engine and tender first past the Down platform is a Class 'S15', whilst an Ivatt 2-6-2T waits in the bay with a branch line service. *2nd September 1962 No. 30925 would be withdrawn by the end of the year but was one of three members of this famous class to escape cutting up. Part of the National Collection, this 4-4-0 has been restored and, in 2015, is to be seen at the Mid Hants Railway. It was the locomotive chosen by the RCTS to grace (as a line drawing) the front cover of the society's house magazine,* The Railway Observer, *from January 1936 until December 1972.*

'THE SOUTH WESTERN LIMITED', 1962

On a rather overcast morning, Norman had come to Sidmouth Junction with Ivo Peters to photograph 'The South Western Limited', a Special which had been organised by the Southern Counties Touring Society. From his elevated position, the signalman watches 'Lord Nelson' Class No. 30861 *Lord Anson* arriving with the SCTS Special, which the 4-6-0 had brought from Waterloo. In the right background, a pair of Class 'M7' 0-4-4Ts wait to take over for the next leg of the itinerary. Ivo can be seen, directly under the loading gauge, hurrying back in order to take more photographs. *2nd September 1962*

The two 0-4-4Ts, No's 30025 and 30024, looking very smart, wait to take the Special forward to Tipton St. Johns and Exmouth, after which it ran alongside the estuary and through Topsham to Exeter Central.

In the meantime, No. 30861 *Lord Anson* had run 'light' to the depot at Exmouth Junction for servicing and turning, ready to return the Special eastwards from Exeter Central, the 4-6-0 working the train as far as Salisbury. Norman and Ivo photographed this return leg at around 2.40pm, at a favourite location – the train entering the cutting leading to the western portal of Honiton Tunnel. The daylight level had not improved from that encountered earlier in the day!

'THE ACE'

'Merchant Navy' No. 35014 *Nederland Line* carefully negotiates the sharply curved approach at the eastern end of Salisbury station, with the Down 'Atlantic Coast Express'. The East signal box – built in 1902 and converted to a flat-roofed structure when the box was modernised in 1928 – can be seen, as too the connection leading from the line serving Platform No. 6 to the short and steeply-graded Market House Branch. *29th September 1962*

The day prior to the scene above, the corresponding Up train starts to gather speed on the 1 in 100 adverse gradient approaching St. James Park Halt. This is all but within sight of Exeter Central, where 'MN' No. 35025 *Brocklebank Line* will have taken over the train. The standard of cleanliness is in contrast to that seen with No. 35014 at Salisbury. *28th September 1962 Note what appears to be an excellent crop of runner beans growing on the lineside allotment, a once familiar feature in the steam era. The concrete fencing visible in the bottom left abuts the ramp at the end of the Down platform at St. James Park Halt.*

ROYAL OBSERVER CORPS

Ivo Peters favourite Bulleid 'light Pacific', No. 34050 *Royal Observer Corps*, comes bounding out from Buckhorn Weston Tunnel and breasts the summit of a stiff eastbound climb. Looking immaculate, the locomotive headed a Special which Norman recorded as bound for Farnborough. This must have been to enable those on board to visit to the famous Air Show (which, that year, ran from 3th to 9th September and was destined to be the last of the annual shows before becoming a biannual event). *9th September 1962* No. 34050 had been presented with the ROC long-service 'ribbon' at a ceremony at Waterloo station on 2nd July in the previous year (1961), the locomotive thereafter carrying (on the cabsides) small plaques in the colours of the medal ribbon awarded to members completing twelve years service. This was, perhaps, somewhat of an afterthought in the case of No. 34050 which, in July 1961, had been in service for fifteen years! Ivo, seen here filming at the side of the track, was a long-standing member of the ROC, serving as a Chief Observer during the Second World War and up until retirement from such duties in 1972. Norman recorded the time of his photograph as 9.20am, so this must have involved an early start from Bath.

Bluebell Railway Visit

A journey was made in Ivo's Bentley in order to photograph (and film) 'The Blue Belle', a Special which had been brought to Haywards Heath from London Victoria behind restored Class 'T9' No. 120. Both photographers were somewhat critical of that rather large headboard! *21st October 1962*
The train was taken forward from Haywards Heath to Horstead Keynes by two Bluebell locomotives, Stroudley 'Terrier' 0-6-0T No. 55 Stepney and Adams radial tank No. 488, the link via Ardingly then still in use by BR for the electric service between Seaford and Horstead Keynes. The two photographers' visit was made just two years after the pioneers of the Bluebell Railway had commenced running a passenger service (the 1960 services at weekends only) between Sheffield Park and Bluebell Halt, a temporary station outside Horstead Keynes. However, as of almost exactly a year before this visit, the Bluebell had negotiated access into Horstead Keynes station.

Now to the Bluebell line; London, Brighton & South Coast Railway Class 'E4' 0-6-2T No. 473 *Birch Grove* heads the Special towards Sheffield Park. Note the plume of exhaust at the rear of the train which, as an operating necessity, was 'topped and tailed'. *21st October 1962*
This radial tank was built at Brighton Works and released into service in 1898. She arrived on the Bluebell as No. 32473 on 16th October 1962, straight out of BR service. Norman's photograph is dated just five days later, which had barely allowed time to paint out the BR emblem and the first two digits of her BR number!

Norman also photographed No. 27 carrying a 'Wealden Rambler' headboard (a title still in use by the railway in 2015) and hauling the restored 4-coach 'Chesham Set' with No. 473 *Birch Grove* bringing up the rear. Hidden by the train in this view is Holywell Halt (also known as Waterworks Halt), which had opened on 1st April 1962 but remained in use for less than two years.

Delivered to the Bluebell as BR No. 31027 in June 1961, for the following two years she carried the name Primrose (and the number 27). In 1963, she was painted in full SE&CR passenger livery. The eldest of the coaches forming the close-coupled set behind No. 27 date from 1898. For some two decades, until 1960, the full set (six – of which the Bluebell purchased four) had been used on the Metropolitan Line's Chesham Branch. The sale price asked by London Transport was £65 each.

After 'The Blue Belle' Special had set off towards Horstead Keynes, No. 120 travelled 'light' to Brighton mpd to be serviced and turned, returning later to Haywards Heath to work the tour back to London. Ivo and Norman also 'popped' down to Brighton, where this photograph was taken of the 4-4-0, now minus that rather conspicuous headboard.

Just as a comparison, here is the same locomotive when still in normal service and carrying her BR number, photographed at Romsey four years earlier. *22nd September 1958*
Initially, No. 30120 (built in 1899) was withdrawn in 1961 but was put aside and taken into Eastleigh Works where, following repair, she was released back into service in L&SWR livery for working both special and ordinary trains. The locomotive was taken out of service again in 1963 but – having been selected for The National Collection – can still be seen today, making appearances at various heritage lines. In 2015, the engine is painted in the early BR lined black livery as seen here at Romsey in 1958.

SOUTHERN FRINGES

BR 'Standard' Class '5' No. 73080, at the head of a perishables train from Weymouth, leaves the line from Yeovil Pen Mill at Castle Cary. This was a former GWR route which, south of Castle Cary, came under the control of the Southern Region from April 1950. It remained thus until all Southern territory west of a line drawn from Wilton, north of Blandford, to Dorchester, was transferred to the Western Region in 1964.

Following arrival with the 'shuttle' service which ran between the Junction and Town stations at Yeovil, Class 'M7' 0-4-4T No. 30129 had eased her two coaches out of the latter station prior to making the next short journey back to the main line. The SR engine shed is just out of sight but the approach and sidings can be seen to the right, along with some motive power stabled between duties. *15th August 1952*
Yeovil Town station had been owned jointly by the GWR and L&SWR. The line westwards to a point just short of Curry Rival Junction, on the GWR's West of England main line, was another branch which passed to the Southern Region of BR in 1950. Eastwards from Yeovil Town, there was also a half-mile link and regular service connecting the Town and Pen Mill stations, the latter still (in 2015) serving Yeovil on the (now singled) Castle Cary-Dorchester line. All were to come/return into WR control from 1964.

SOUTHAMPTON CENTRAL – 3

In the foreword to this book, an explanation was given as to why Norman returned time and time again to certain locations. Southampton Central was one such firm favourite, especially the western end where that impressive signal gantry could be included. Also, as someone (other than when in the company of Ivo Peters) who relied on public transport, Southampton was an easy place to reach by train from Norman's home in Bath – not that getting anywhere appeared to have served as much of a deterrent, judging from some of the places he succeded in reaching by a combination of train, bus and on foot!

No. 82014, a BR 'Standard' Class '3' 2-6-2T built at Swindon in 1952 for the Southern Region and here allocated to Eastleigh, heads a train of empty tankers which were being returned to the oil refinery at Fawley. Note the customary barrier wagons immediately behind the locomotive, although judging from other photographs, it was unusual to find a van included for such a purpose. *27th September 1962*

A brace of 'rebuilds'. 'West Country' Class No. 34012 *Launceston* departs from Platform 3 with a Brighton-Plymouth service which, at this time, was still being worked throughout by the same steam locomotive, making this the longest continuous working on the Southern Region. In the adjacent Platform 4, the tender of No. 34037 *Clovelly* is being replenished before the 'light Pacific' continues westwards with a Waterloo to Weymouth train. *4th October 1962*
Both locomotives had been recent reallocations; No. 34012 to Brighton (from Bricklayer Arms) in early July and No. 34037 to Eastleigh (from Bournemouth) in late September '62 and yet to receive a '71A' shedplate.

THE 'PINES EXPRESS'

The 'Pines Express' – mention this famous cross-country train and most enthusiasts will immediately associate the title with the 'Somerset & Dorset' line but, after the 'Pines' (and all through summer Saturday traffic) was diverted away from the S&D in early-September 1962, the 'named' service continued to run, now via Southampton and Oxford. 'West Country' Class No. 34103 *Calstock*, carrying the WR-style headboard as used for the last runs before the service had been diverted, restarts the 'Pines' from its scheduled call at Southampton. *4th October 1962*

I selected this photograph from a choice of several featuring this famous – but now diverted – named train because the fireman, seen looking from the cab, is Aubry Punter, who had fired to Peter Smith on the last Up 'Pines Express' via the S&D just a month earlier. His driver here is Jim Tranter. Branksome based men still worked the 'Pines' (now between Bournemouth and Oxford) but, from the start of the following year, the former S&D outpost was closed and the men transferred to Bournemouth mpd.

Scheduled and Special Traffic on Honiton Bank

Racing out of the eastern end of Honiton Tunnel, No. 34109 *Sir Trafford Leigh Mallory* is in charge of a Plymouth-Waterloo express, which the rebuilt 'Battle of Britain' had taken control of from Exeter Central. *23rd September 1963 Although only fifteen summers had passed since No. 34109 (the penultimate member of the class) was released into traffic, the locomotive had already been rebuilt, early in 1961, and yet would remain in traffic for just another twelve months after Norman took this photograph.*

Norman Lockett returned to a favourite length of lineside to photograph L&NER Class 'A4' No. 60022 *Mallard*, when this famous locomotive made a return visit to the West Country. The purpose was to commemorite the passage of fifteen years since this Gresley 'Pacific' was involved in the Locomotive Exchanges, which included services between London, Exeter and Plymouth, in 1948. Here the 'Streak' climbs the incline from Seaton Junction to Honiton Tunnel with the LCGB 'West Countryman' Railtour'. *24th February 1963*

'THE HAMPSHIRE VENTURER' RAILTOUR

Restored Drummond Class 'T9' 4-4-0 No. 120 features again, the choice of the Southern Counties Touring Society for two legs of 'The Hampshire Venturer' railtour, including the initial run from London Victoria as far as Andover Junction. It is at the latter location she is featured here, about to enter the station whilst passing the branch connection to Andover Town, Winchester and Shawford Junction, curving away sharply to the right. *10th March 1963*

Quite by chance I came across a very similar view of this scene (attributed to another fine railway photographer, Anthony Richardson) in the May 1963 issue of the Railway Magazine. *So we emailed a scan of Norman's photograph to Anthony, who was able to identify easily that he was indeed one of the lineside photographer's seen above (the one with the 'shock of blonde hair' in the right background!).*

Having continued from Andover to Salisbury, including a foray along the line to Bulford Camp and back (all undertaken behind other motive power), No. 120 took over the Special again as far as Southampton Docks. From the Eastern Dock, 'USA' Class 0-6-0T No. 30074 worked the SCTS train to Fawley, then back to Eastleigh and is seen here near Marchwood on the outbound run along the branch from Totton. *10th March 1963*

This visit to the Talbot Heath area of Bournemouth was a little farther west towards Gas Works Junction than the location more usually chosen by Norman. In the distance, beyond the Rothesay Road overbridge, are the Down Distant signals for Gas Works Junction; the left arm (as viewed here) is for the line towards Branksome station, the other towards Bournemouth West. BR 'Standard' Class '4' 2-6-0 No. 76005 heads a service which Norman described as Waterloo to Weymouth but was, perhaps, the Weymouth portion of a Waterloo to Bournemouth West service, which had been detached at Bournemouth Central. *9th June 1963*

Class 'M7' 0-4-4T No. 30127 pulls out a rake of empty stock from No. 5 platform at Bournemouth West. *9th June 1963*
This member of the class was a favourite choice and saw regular use for 'station pilot' duties at Bournemouth West. It was built in 1911 and provided with a steam reverser; a feature much appreciated (especially on summer Saturdays) when constant changes between fore and back gear were necessary to bring and (as seen here) remove empty stock from the various platforms. Summer 1963 was to prove the last before No. 30127 and the few other examples of these elderly 0-4-4Ts remaining at Bournemouth were withdrawn.

BOURNEMOUTH WEST DEPARTURES

With a good head of steam, 'Battle of Britain' Class No. 34087 *145 Squadron* commences the journey to Waterloo as it negotiates the various sets of points leading from Platform No. 6 towards the Up Main line. *9th June 1963*

Bournemouth West station was closed on 4th October 1965, although passenger services had actually been withdrawn as a temporary measure on 6th September during the electrification of the main line, with a bus service being substituted in its place. The station building was demolished shortly after the closure was made permanent. When this writer last visited the site of it in the 1980s, the only thing remaining as recognisable was the Midland Hotel; the prominent building on the skyline immediately beyond the station. Much more recently, the hotel has been converted to create private flats which rejoice in the name of 'Midland Heights'!

This departure from Platform No. 1 features another well-groomed original example of the 'Battle of Britain' Class, No. 34061 *73 Squadron*. Note that the train reporting number on the smokebox door is chalked up as 3.15pm. *23rd June 1963*

HAYLING ISLAND BRANCH

Norman, with Ivo, had made a brief visit to the 4½ mile branch line from Havant to Hayling Island in 1959. Now listed for closure (this before the publication of *The Beeching Report – The Reshaping of British Railways*, issued on 27th March 1963), the two photographers decided it was time to pay another visit: Norman to photograph the diminutive Stroudley 'Terrier' 0-6-0Ts which worked the branch, whilst Ivo also wished to record the line on 16mm colour film. In the event, they finished up making two visits before the line was closed.

No. 32650, built at Brighton in 1876, sets off from Havant, rounding the sharp curve and over a level crossing, bound for Hayling Island, a journey which, with two intermediate stops, usually occupied thirteen minutes (ten minutes if non-stop). In later years, the leading van was provided for passenger luggage and prams, apparently carried in large numbers on Saturdays during the height of the holiday season. *28th July 1963*
The 'A1' Class 'Terriers' were rebuilt from 1911 onwards and redesignated as 'A1X' Class, No. 650 (as it then was) being outshopped in May 1920. The engine twice carried names, beginning life as LB&SCR No. 650 Whitechapel and later working on the Isle of Wight as No. W9 Fishbourne, before becoming BR No. 32650 from November 1953. Following withdrawal, No. 32650 was sold for intended exhibit outside a new Civic Centre at Sutton. However, supposedly until the building project was complete, the 0-6-0 went on loan, to be looked after by the Kent & East Sussex Railway. In the event it remained based there and was restored to working order but, more recently, it has moved to the Spa Valley Railway where, in 2015, it was again being overhauled.

OPPOSITE PAGE TOP: This is farther around the bend leading away southwards from the main line station at Havant. Someone had been brandishing a paint brush on the front of No. 32646 (built in 1876) to brighten up her appearance! The spark arrester fitted to the chimneys of these locomotives was a precaution against setting fire to Langston Bridge, a 1,000ft-long wooden structure that carried the line between the mainland and Hayling Island, which included a swing section for the passage of sea craft. It was the severe weight restriction placed upon the use of the bridge which necessitated the retension of the elderly but lightweight 'Terrier' 0-6-0Ts for work on this line. *1st September 1963*
This locomotive is also still extant, restored and in working order. Since withdrawn from service by BR, the ongoing 'career' of this 0-6-0T has included static display outside a pub named 'The Hayling Billy'. Nowadays she can be seen at work on the Isle of Wight Steam Railway, having regained the number W8 and the name Freshwater, as carried during service in Southern Railway days.

OPPOSITE PAGE BOTTOM: No. 32670 bustles along the branch, nearing Langston* whilst heading for Hayling. *28th July 1963*
* Langston (no 'e') was the spelling adopted by the railway, although Langstone (with the 'e') was apparently as it was spelled by everybody else.
Yet another of this class which, since withdrawal by BR, has been restored and is working as No. 3 Bodiam (a name previously carried for a part of its long career before withdrawn by BR) on the Kent & East Sussex Railway who, along with the Terrier Trust, owns the locomotive.

No. 32670 features again, here having just set off from Langston station and passing the fixed Distant signal for Langston Bridge. The post also carried – for traffic in the opposite direction – the Up Home signal protecting Langston Crossing, which was sited adjacent to the single platform station. *1st September 1963*
Much of the route of the former branch line has become the 'Hayling Billy Trail', a part of National Cycle Network Route 2. More recently this has been incorporated into a long-distance footpath known as the 'Shipwright's Way'.

No. 32650 draws closer to the northern end of Langston Bridge, passing behind the gardens of properties fronting the west side of Langstone Road. The points served a siding, which terminated approximately where the Langstone Sailing Club now stands to the north end of the road bridge linking with the island. *28th July 1963*
The property seen in the right background, with the distinctive four chimneys and a small flat-roofed area decorated with iron crestings, can still be easily identified when passing along Langstone Road.

This is a scene from an earlier visit. No. 32661, on its way towards Hayling Island, had just crossed Langston Bridge (left background) and was approaching the single wooden platform at North Hayling, positioned at a rather remote and exposed point on the line. *16th October 1959*
The signal, the arm of which is just visible in the 'clear' position beyond the rear of the train, was operated from the signal box seen perched on the bridge. This box was in use only when it became necessary to operate the swing section of the bridge, for the passage of a vessel wishing to pass between the waters of Langstone and Hayling harbours. Such bridge swings required the appropriate rail signals being placed to danger and the connecting wires temporarily disconnected. Shimmering in the bright autumnal sunlight, the concrete bridge providing road access to the island can be seen to the right. This structure (opened in 1956) replaced the wooden toll bridge which had been owned by the railway.

No. 32650 approaches the small terminus at Hayling Island. *1st September 1963*
The branch line closed to passenger traffic just nine weeks after Norman took this photograph. No. 32650 hauled the last public passenger train to leave the terminus on Saturday, 2nd November 1963 but a Special, organised by the LCGB, visited the line the following day. All of the 0-6-0Ts working services on the Hayling Island Branch were withdrawn following its closure.

AN S&D INTERLUDE

Originally purchased on a long lease held jointly by the Midland Railway and the L&SWR, even after Nationalisation in 1948, the S&D line remained associated with the Southern Region of BR. Admittedly, towards the end of the 1950s and into the '60s, the Western Region gradually gained ever more control, their

boundary eventually stretching southwards to just a mile or so north of Blandford Forum. However, there is enough justification for including just a few views of the 'bottom half' of the S&D main line and should you want more, we refer you to the first book in this series, *The Somerset & Dorset Railway 1935-1966*.

Despite the withdrawal of the 'Pines Express' and all summer Saturday through holiday traffic, a few excursions continued to run from Bristol and Bath, via the S&D line, to Poole and Bournemouth. This is one such example, an August Bank Holiday Monday excursion. Bath-allocated BR Class '5' No. 73047 drops down the gradient on the approach to Blandford Forum station. Note the pouch containing the tablet for the single line section from Shillingstone, extended ready for collection from the lineside mechanical 'catcher'. The Up Starting signal, to the left, was provided with 'co-acting' arms, because a footbridge over the line (which still survives and from which position Norman photographed this scene) made sighting of the lower arm difficult for a faster non-stopping service. On the left is the water tank, on a substantial stone base, whilst the siding in the right foreground gave access to a loading dock. *5th August 1963*

OPPOSITE PAGE TOP: Following the cessation of the summer Saturday traffic, the use of a Bulleid 'light Pacific' on normal service trains over the S&D became a relatively rare occurance. This sighting of Bournemouth's No. 34103 *Calstock*, on the 4.21 semi-fast from Bath, was the consequence of having to make a late substitution for the allocated locomotive, a BR Standard Class '4', on an earlier Up train. This is the scene looking northwards from an overbridge at Horsington a little to the north of Templecombe. *5th August 1963*

OPPOSITE PAGE BOTTOM: Immediately to the south of the previous image, as viewed in the opposite direction, BR 'Standard' Class '5' No. 73052 heads towards Wincanton with the 3.40pm Bournemouth West to Bristol Temple Meads, which included mail traffic detached at Mangotsfield and shunted onto the Bristol-North of England mail train. The lineside bush in the background masks all except the chimney of the railway cottage at Horsington Crossing, once also the site of Templecombe No. 3 Junction signal box. The gantry to the rear of the train supported the signals controlling access into Templecombe Lower Yard and mpd. *5th August 1963*

Just to conclude this brief interlude of a favourite line, this 'Somerset & Dorset' Special – organised by the Home Counties Railway Society – brought together a final pairing of these two locomotives, both built for the S&DJR. Class '7F' 2-8-0 No. 53807 and Class '4F' 0-6-0 No. 44558 (originally S&DJR No's 87 and 58) come romping downhill from the summit at Milldown, north of Blandford Forum, where, on reaching the foot of the descent, they head northwards through the pastoral delights of the Stour Valley. *7th June 1964*

No. 53807, the last of this famous class to remain in use on the S&D, made a final run, with a Bath-Evercreech North Yard freight, on 5th September 1964. She returned to Bath with just a brake van in tow, following which she was taken out of service. No. 44558 was withdrawn in December 1964.

I couldn't resist including this image as a 'two pager'. Norman and Ivo were chasing the Special northwards in anticipation that they might obtain at least one photograph and for Ivo to film the train before it reached the northern half of the line, where it was likely to be greeted by an 'invasion' of enthusiasts (as in fact happened). The itinerary also included a return run along the Evercreech Junction-Highbridge line. The tour had commenced at Waterloo but returned to Paddington, after following the ex-Midland main line north from Bristol to Gloucester and then heading south again along ex-GWR metals through Stroud and the Golden Valley to Swindon.

MILBORNE PORT

With the autumn shadows already lengthening, unrebuilt 'Battle of Britain' Class No. 34075 *264 Squadron* restarts a Down local service following a brief pause at Milborne Port. This little station had already been reduced in status to Milborne Port Halt, its booking office closed and tickets sold from the signal box until this, too, closed in 1965. Note the sidings had already been taken out. *12th October 1963*

Earlier that same afternoon, rebuilt 'West Country' Class No. 34014 *Budleigh Salterton* **looked to be in fine external condition as she headed south-westwards towards Sherborne with a Templecombe to Exeter train.** *12th October 1963*

This was a return visit by Norman, after a gap of more than a decade, to the lineside about 1¼ miles south-west of Milborne Port station. It is, in fact, the view as seen looking in the opposite direction at or immediately adjacent to the same overbridge from which the photograph on page 27 was taken. In 1950, Norman must have reached this location by public transport and on foot; this time it was in Ivo Peters' Bentley. They both returned here a few more times but for those visits it appears that Norman was using a 35mm camera with colour transparency film.

Mention of Budleigh Salterton, as the name of the Bulleid 'light Pacific' seen in the previous caption, provides a somewhat tenuous link to the town of that name, in order to feature this diminutive locomotive, an oil-fired 0-4-0 built in 1916 by the Avonside Engine Company at Bristol for the Royal Arsenal at Woolwich (hence the name). *23rd September 1963*

Woolwich was purchased for a new 18 inch gauge line laid out in the gardens of Bicton House, near Budleigh Salterton, and opened on 6th April 1963. Norman and Ivo Peters decided to pay a visit whilst the pair were en route to the lineside close to Honiton Tunnel. The locomotive is still to be found at what, nowadays, is known as the Bicton Woodlands Railway, which forms an attraction within the impressive Bicton Park Botanical Gardens.

SEMLEY

Rebuilt 'West Country' No. 34032 *Camelford* **approaches Semley station and the summit of the four-mile eastbound climb from Gillingham, which lifts the line out of the Blackmoor Vale. The train, the 9.03am local service from Templecombe to Salisbury, was about to pass under the three-arch bridge carrying the A350 road about 2½ miles north of Shaftesbury. Semley station was a railhead for Shaftesbury and, for many decades until the late-1950s, a bus service linked the two.** *5th August 1963*

SECTION 5
THE MID-SIXTIES
WILTON SOUTH

On an overcast day, modified 'Battle of Britain' Class No. 34077 *603 Squadron* approaches the station with a Waterloo-Plymouth train. *21st March 1964*
The siding immediately to the right of the train was used, during the era of the 'Devon Belle', to hold the locomotive waiting to take over the famous (albeit short-lived) Pullman express for the onwards journey to the west. The service was advertised to the public as non-stop between Waterloo and Seaton Junction. A similar unadvertised change of locomotive was undertaken here for the corresponding Up train. The trees in the left background stand on an embankment beyond which lies the former GWR cross-country line towards Warminster and Westbury. This ran parallel with the SR route for the first couple of miles north-west from Salisbury, until the SR turned away towards the south-west, around the curved formation seen above. In 1973, the ex-GWR line was connected into the Southern route a little to the east of Wilton, since when all traffic has used the latter tracks.

Wilton South station from the footbridge, with 'West Country' No. 34100 *Appledore* in charge of another express bound for Plymouth and observing the permanent speed restriction imposed around the sharply-curved approach to the station. *21st March 1964*

In the post-Second World War steam era, this permanent speed restriction was the last such constraint encountered on the main running lines until approaching Exeter. This made it a very popular route with train-timers and photographers alike. This station gained the suffix 'South' only after Nationalisation of the railways, presumably to differentiae from the nearby station on the ex-GWR line, which became Wilton North. However, the latter closed on 19th September 1955, whilst Wilton South survived for passenger traffic until 7th March 1966.

Some eighteen months earlier and with far better weather conditions, this view westwards from the footbridge finds Exmouth Junction-allocated No. 34074 *46 Squadron* arriving with the weekdays 6.15am Plymouth-Salisbury, a service which called at every* intermediate station and halt, and was scheduled to take 3hrs 22mins to complete its journey. *29th September 1962*

The three-coach set bringing up the rear of the train is crossing, in turn, the bridges over the River Wylye and the A36 road; the Down platform was accessable from the road via the footpath seen on the left.

Just beyond Wilton, the line commenced a climb of some eighteen miles, all the way to Semley.

* *Tamerton Foliot was the sole exception shown in the SR Passenger Time Table – that was because the station had been closed the previous year but its name not yet removed from the time table!*

BR 'Britannia' 4-6-2 No. 70020 *Mercury* draws away from the Waterloo-Salisbury main line at the site of the former Red Post Junction, two miles west of Andover. The section remaining open to Ludgershall extends for less than six miles northwards from Red Post. *8th March 1964*

The 'South Western Rambler'

This railtour was organised by the Southern Counties Touring Society and included a run along a part of the former Midland & South Western Junction route from Andover (Red Post Junction) north as far as Ludgershall. By the date of the tour in 1964, this railhead was retained purely for military traffic, as it still is today.

Following the return to the main line, the SCTS Special continued westwards and is seen here passing through Grateley station. No. 70020 remained in charge until reaching Salisbury. The station is still open today but has lost all of the buildings seen here and its sidings.

From Salisbury the special was taken forward to Templecombe by BR Class '9F' 2-10-0 No. 92209 and, following a double reversal of direction, along the southern section of the S&D to Broadstone. Then to Hamworthy Junction (featured here), where another reversal of direction was necessary. *8th March 1964*
I suspect Norman had hoped to obtain an image of the locomotive unfettered by other photographers but decided this was as good as it would get.

'One man and his dog!' The time taken in 'running round' its train provided ample opportunity to take another shot before the 2-10-0 set off on the next leg across Holes Bay to Poole, then to Bournemouth Central. Meanwhile, No. 70020 had run 'light' from Salisbury to Bournemouth to take over from No. 92209 and complete the run back to London.
Not the usual style of picture from Norman but I suppose one might argue that it was not every day you could witness a BR 'Nine' working a passenger train whilst running tender first.

Previously in these pages, No. 30850 *Lord Nelson* was featured arriving at Swindon Works with an enthusiasts special. Here, it was the turn for a visit by No. 34038 *Lynton* with 'The East Midlander' railtour' (one of several occasions this title was used by the RCTS). Following arrival and having being turned, the 'West Country' was eased back to pass over the Rodbourne Road underbridge. The tall building was the pattern Shop (surmounted with large water tanks) whilst in the right background is 'J' Shop, which housed the Iron Shop. *9th May 1964*
This tour commenced from Nottingham, travelling via Leicester and Banbury to Didcot. From there No. 34038 was used for the next stages to Eastleigh (for a works visit) and return to Swindon (out via Winchester Chesil and back via Salisbury and Westbury). Two works visits in the same day made this a very popular tour. At Swindon No. 34038 handed over to ex-LM&SR No. 46251 City of Nottingham for the return home.

OFF THEIR BEATEN TRACKS

Another tour which provided the opportunity to visit the works at both Swindon and Eastleigh was organised by the Warwickshire Railway Society. Motive power throughout was Gresley Class 'A3' Pacific No. 4472 *Flying Scotsman*. This had been withdrawn by BR the previous year but purchased by Alan Peglar and restored at Darlington, as closely as was possible, to its L&NER livery and condition. Having set off from Eastleigh at the start of the return to Saltley, No. 4472 passes through Micheldever in the early evening, heading for Basingstoke before veering northwards from the SR main line and heading towards Reading. *16th August 1964*

EASTER MONDAY DEPARTURES

'West Country' Class No. 34045 *Ottery St Mary* departs from Platform 5 at Bournemouth West with a train for Waterloo. In the foreground stands that most respected of drivers, Donald Beale, with whom Norman had occasionally riden on the footplate over the S&D line, doubtless arranged via the Bath Shedmaster Harold Morris and their mutual friend Ivo Peters! *30th March 1964*
It was most unusual for Norman to take a photograph looking towards the right-hand side of any train departing from Platforms 5 or 6 here, so in this image we can see a slightly different background which includes a rare view of the Bournemouth West goods yard. Donald stands by the water column serving 'No. 6 Road'.

Reverting to the camera position more usually adopted by Norman, 'Merchant Navy' No. 35026 *Lamport & Holt Line***, then only recently transferred to Nine Elms, pulls away from Platform 4 with the Up 'Bournemouth Belle'.** *30th March 1964*

This appears to be the first occasion Norman photographed at this location when steam was outnumbered by newer forms of motive power; note the 'Hampshire' DEMU and the 'Crompton' Type 2. The writer retains personal memories of Bournemouth West, having arrived at the terminus for his honeymoon (travelling via the Somerset & Dorset of course!) and, some years after the station had been demolished, filming with Peter Smith the final sequence for the BBC documentary All change at Evercreech Junction.

BANK HOLIDAY TRAFFIC
ON PARKSTONE BANK

An August Bank Holiday Monday excursion via the Somerset & Dorset line nears the summit of Parkstone Bank behind Bath-based BR Class '5' 4-6-0 No. 73051. 3rd August 1964
As will be evident from this and the following view, this was a section of lineside much appreciated by both Norman and Ivo, offering the opportunity to photograph hard-working locomotives in an attractive setting. However, by 1964, the occasional excursion, enthusiasts or school special reaching Bournemouth via the S&D route served only as a sad reminder of the volumes of holiday traffic which had passed over this line until just a couple of summers earlier.

Stanier Class '8F' 2-8-0 No. 48470 (built by the GWR for the LM&SR at Swindon in 1944) was an unusual choice of locomotive for this working, the 6.55am stopping service from Bath, Green Park. However, by the following year, when the fate of the S&D line was sealed and the motive power availability at Bath had so deteriorated, the use of these 2-8-0s became – of necessity – a more frequent occurance. *3rd August 1964*

A Mystery Resolved

Rebuilt 'West Country' No. 34046 *Braunton* heads a Bournemouth Central-Weymouth train beneath Glenferness Avenue Bridge and towards Gas Works Junction. *30th August 1964*
The large sign facing the railway at the top of the cutting appears in several of Norman's photographs and I was intrigued to know what appeared thereon, obviously designed to attract the attention of passing rail travellers. By the marvels of digital technology, I have been able to 'turn' the image sufficient to discover that it reads 'Talbot Heath School Playing Field'. The sign no longer exists but the educational establishment it advertised does; it's the former Bournemouth Girls High School, renamed when it transferred to the Talbot Heath site in 1936. The choice of this photograph was also influenced by the motive power – this example having been restored in much more recent times from little more than a 'heap of scrap' to present day (2015) main line running standards.

ISLE OF WIGHT – 2

From the 14th to 16th July 1964, Norman and Ivo Peters paid another visit to the Isle of Wight system. As was the case for their previous visit in 1961, they spent most of their time at the lineside between Ryde St. John's Road and in the vicinity of Smallbrook Junction.

Setting off from Ryde St. John's Road station, Class 'O2' No. W24 *Calbourne* is at the head of a train for Cowes. *16th July 1964*

Situated 1¼ miles from Ryde Pier Head, this was the location of the island's railway workshops, a part of which can be seen far right. The vehicle also seen to the right in this and the following photographs was a Riding, Mess & Stores Van, used as part of the Works train.

The same location as viewed from the Up side of the running lines. Pulling away from the station, Class 'O2' No. W21 *Sandown* passes the signal box also with a train for Cowes. *14th July 1964*

Heading away from Ryde St. John's Road towards Smallbrook Junction, No. W20 *Shanklin* has a route disc missing but the position of the one to be seen confirms this as yet another Cowes line train. *14th July 1964*
The feature prominent on the skyline in this and some of Norman's other photographs taken hereabouts is the spire of Ryde Holy Trinity Parish Church.

Just a few yards farther south and, again, Norman had moved across to the Down side of the line. No. W30 *Shorwell* appears to be in fine external condition with yet another Cowes line train. Note that the fireman has spotted Norman. *16th July 1964*

SMALLBROOK JUNCTION

Having just passed beneath the bridge carrying Smallbrook Lane over the railway, No. W26 *Whitwell* approaches Smallbrook Junction, where the lines to Cowes and Ventnor went there separate ways.
15th July 1964

At the junction, No. W28 *Ashey* takes the line towards Brading with a train ultimately bound for Ventnor. Once each holiday season was over, the signal box here was closed, the points were clipped and all signal arms taken down and stored until the following summer. For the rest of the year, as mentioned earlier, the two lines from Ryde St. Johns Road were worked as separate single track routes, with the sections extending westwards to Haven Street and southwards to Brading respectively.
15th July 1964

With the shadows lengthening, No. W17 *Seaview* swings across onto the line towards Ashey, with a train to Newport and Cowes. *15th July 1964*

The small signal box at Smallbrook can be seen at the rear of this Newport and Cowes line train. The locomotive this time is No. W18 *Ningwood*. There was a wooden platform at the far end of the signal box, which extended to both lines and enabled signalman and footplate crew to exchange the single line tokens as the trains passed by without stopping.

Here, nowadays, is the eastern end of the Isle of Wight Steam Railway, with an interconnecting platform also served by the Island Line's public trains which run only between Ryde Pier Head and Shanklin. Hopefully, it may not be too many more years before the steam railway is extended along the section featured in these photographs, as far as Ryde St. John's Road.

Norman travelled across to Ventnor, where for some reason he appears to have taken only this single monocrome photograph of No. W35 *Freshwater* which, having just emerged from the tunnel under St. Boniface Down, is seen arriving with a train from **Ryde Pier Head.**

Note not a single locomotive has been featured more than once in recalling this visit to the Island!

HONITON TUNNEL – THE EASTERN EXIT

This end, perhaps less frequently visited by photographers during the steam era than the other portal, emerged into an extremely picturesque cutting at the head of Honiton Bank or, as it was sometimes known, Seaton Bank – perhaps to distinquish it from the incline leading to the western (Honiton) end of the tunnel.

David Lockett retains a vivid memory of his earliest visit here, accompanying his father and – whilst walking across the fields from one end of the tunnel to reach the other – coming 'under attack' by a flock of turkeys: "*They frightened the living daylights out of me; thankfully Dad succeeded in 'shooing' them away whilst I made my escape!*"

Rebuilt 'West Country' No. 34005 *Barnstaple* provides rather an excess of power for this Exeter Central to Chard Junction two-coach local.

'Battle of Britain' No. 34054 *Lord Beaverbrook* emerges into bright sunshine at the head of a Torrington-Waterloo train. *Both 22nd August 1964*

This must rank amongst the finest of images to feature this location. Modified 'BB' No. 34089 *602 Squadron* climbs the final stretch of 1 in 80 in fine style with the 10.35am (SO) Waterloo to Padstow. Note the colour-light signal at the side of the Up line, visible above the rear coaches of the train. *22nd August 1964*

This was destined to be the last month of the final summer before the Western Region, having been allocated operational control of the line westwards from Wilton with effect from 1st January 1963, withdrew through summer services via this main line route to Exeter. Thereafter, with many of the smaller intermediate stations closing in March 1966, effectively this became a secondary route.

TRAFFIC VARIETY AT SOUTHAMPTON CENTRAL

With only 'one board off' for the route ahead, 'West Country' No. 34002 *Salisbury* runs slowly through Southampton Central and past the signal box with a Down freight including empty oil tanks bound for the refinery at Fawley. *28th September 1964*

Norman was back the following day to photograph the same service, this time hauled by one of the rebuilt 'light Pacifics', 'BB' Class No. **34087** *145 Squadron*. *29th September 1964*
The impressive signal box was opened in 1935, replacing one at the opposite end of the station which had also controlled the level crossing that had been superceded by the road bridge.

Norman took very few photographs of Up trains from platform level at Southampton Central, preferring instead the elevated position (as seen elsewhere in this book) from the public footbridge at the east end of the station. Here is a rare exception, with 'MN' No. 35026 *Lamport & Holt Line* arriving at Platform 1 with a Weymouth-Waterloo service. *29th September 1964*

'THE EAST DEVON' RAILTOUR

At Axminster, the 'MN' sets off for Seaton Junction whilst Ivatt 2-6-2T No. 41291 stands at the head of the 'supplementary' train waiting in the bay platform, destined for Lyme Regis. This train was 'tailed' by another of the Ivatt 2-6-2Ts, No. 41206, the presence of which is betrayed by the steam seen above the second coach of the main train. 7th March 1965

This railtour, organised by the LCGB, was first run on 28th February 1965 and repeated a week later on Sunday 7th March. The same motive power was used on both dates. 'Merchant Navy' Class No. 35022 *Holland-America Line* brought the Special from Waterloo to Axminster. Here there was the option to leave the main train for a supplementary trip to Lyme Regis and back, then down the main line to Seaton Junction, for a return trip over the Seaton Branch. Next, on down the main line to Sidmouth

Junction for a trip to Sidmouth and back as far as Tipton St. Johns. There, the travellers rejoined the stock of the main train (which had also paid a visit to Sidmouth) and continued, via Exmouth, to Exeter Central. Meanwhile, No. 35022, had worked 'light engine' from Seaton Junction to Exeter for servicing and turning in order to return the Special to Waterloo. Only an enthusiast could have prepared such an itinerary complete with options!

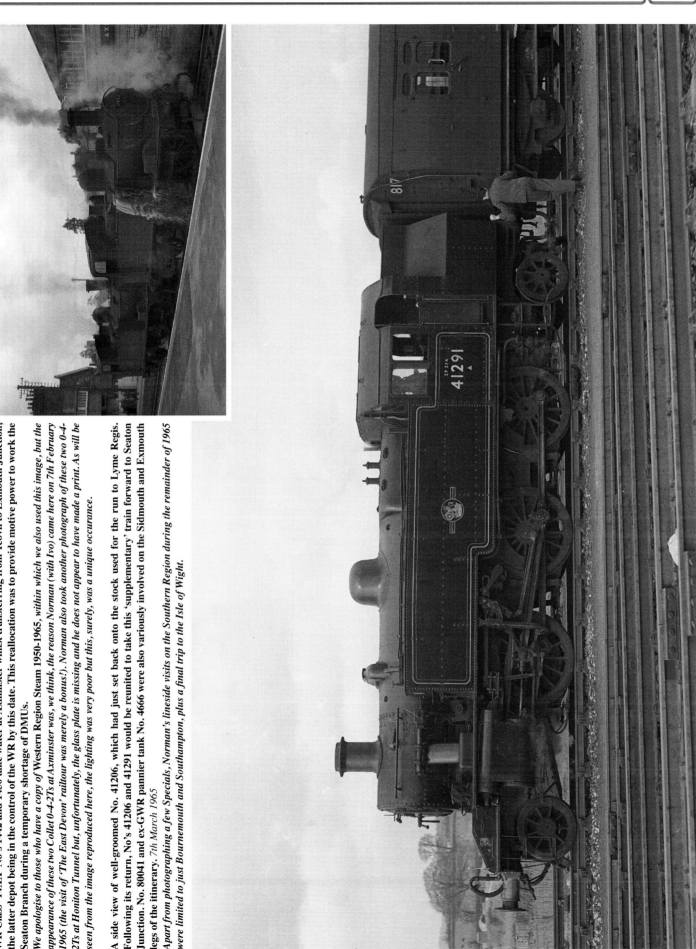

WR Class '14XX' No's 1442 and 1450 take water at Axminster whilst transferring from Yeovil to Exmouth Junction, the latter depot being in the control of the WR by this date. This reallocation was to provide motive power to work the Seaton Branch during a temporary shortage of DMUs.

We apologise to those who have a copy of Western Region Steam 1950-1965, within which we also used this image, but the appearance of these two Collet 0-4-2Ts at Axminster was, we think, the reason Norman (with 1vo) came here on 7th February 1965 (the visit of 'The East Devon' railtour was merely a bonus!). Norman also took another photograph of these two 0-4-2Ts at Honiton Tunnel but, unfortunately, the glass plate is missing and he does not appear to have made a print. As will be seen from the image reproduced here, the lighting was very poor but this, surely, was a unique occurance.

A side view of well-groomed No. 41206, which had just set back onto the stock used for the run to Lyme Regis. Following its return, No's 41206 and 41291 would be reunited to take this 'supplementary' train forward to Seaton Junction. No. 80041 and ex-GWR pannier tank No. 4666 were also variously involved on the Sidmouth and Exmouth legs of the itinerary. *7th March 1965*

Apart from photographing a few Specials, Norman's lineside visits on the Southern Region during the remainder of 1965 were limited to just Bournemouth and Southampton, plus a final trip to the Isle of Wight.

'THE WEALDSMAN' RAILTOUR

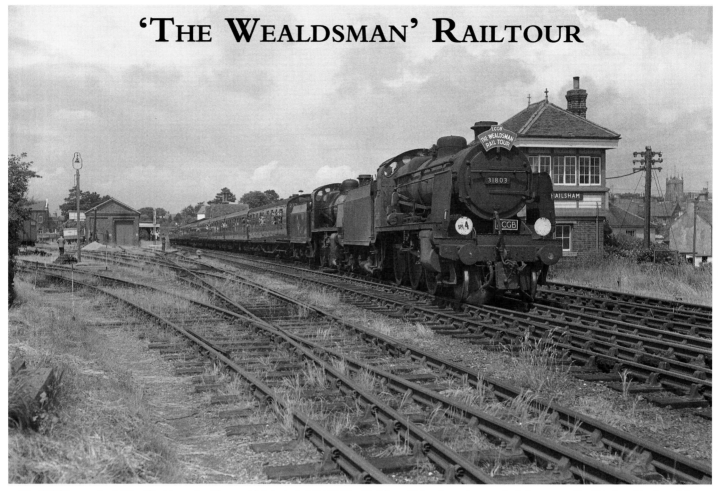

The LCGB organised 'The Wealdsman' railtour, which included the Eridge-Hailsham-Polegate route, popularly known as the 'Cuckoo Line', and (see below) the Horsham-Guildford branch, referred to as the 'Cranleigh Line', to run on the day following closure of both to public passenger services on 12th June 1965. Seen leaving Hailsham behind 'U' Class No. 31803 and 'N' Class No. 31411, this pair of Maunsell 'Moguls' had taken over the train from No. 34050 *Royal Observer Corps* at Three Bridges, following the run from Waterloo via Horsham. *13th June 1965*

By the early evening, the Special had reached Horsham for a second time, behind unmodified 'light Pacific' No. 34050 *Royal Observer Corps*, which had taken over from the pair of 'Moguls' at Haywards Heath. Following a reversal of direction at Horsham, this pair of Bulleid Class 'Q1' 0-6-0s, No's 33027 and 33006, took the train along the 'Cranleigh Line' to Guildford, then back to London. Confirmation of the exact location featured here would be appreciated.

In between following progress of 'The Wealdsman' tour, it appears Norman and Ivo paid a brief visit to the Bluebell Railway because here, dated the same day, is a photograph taken of 4-4-0 No. 9017 *Earl of Berkeley*, resplendent following completion of a repaint to GWR livery. Tucked in behind the 'Dukedog' (which had arrived on the Bluebell in September 1962) is former L&SWR radial tank 4-4-2 No. 488.

BOURNEMOUTH CENTRAL – EASTBOUND ARRIVALS AND DEPARTURES

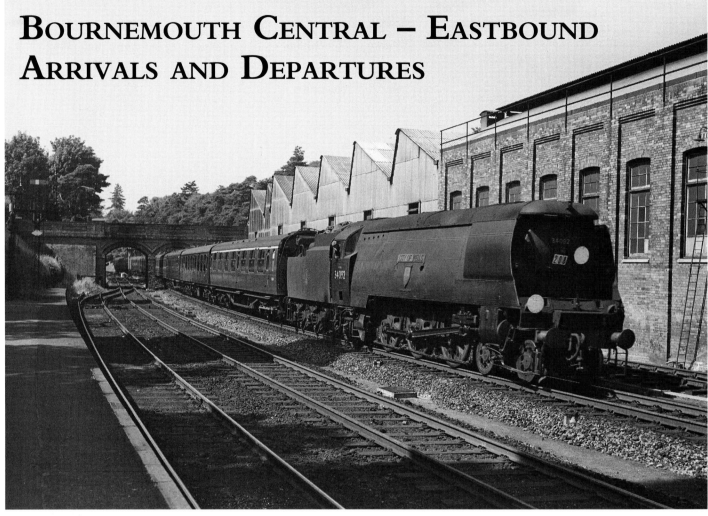

During the 1960s, most of Norman's photographic visits to Bournemouth, often made on a Sunday, were to the lineside around Talbot and at Bournemouth West, rather than here at the imposing Central station.

'West Country' Class No. 34092 *City of Wells* approaches the Up platform, passing the side of the motive power depot. Norman recorded the train as the 10.44am (Sundays) Weymouth to Bournemouth. The '208' duty number carried might well refer to a previous working by No. 34092. *30th August 1964 The overbridge carries Beechey Road across the rails. Otherwise, a very different background is to be found here today; the land formerly occupied by the mpd is now a large car park, the level of which has been raised to be nearly as high as the bottom of the windows seen in this 1965 view.*

'Battle of Britain' Class No. 34076 *41 Squadron* sets off in the sunshine with the 2.10pm (Sundays) departure for Waterloo. This locomotive was shortly to make a final transfer from Eastleigh to Salisbury from where, in January 1966, it was withdrawn. *10th October 1965 The background here today is also much changed. The site of the large building seen on the right is now occupied by a 'Homebase' store. The rather neglected station roof (note the absence of much of the glazing), was further damaged during the 'great storm' in 1987. However, work undertaken from 2000, transformed the glazed roof and end screens, so as to closely resemble what, I suspect, had been the objective of the original design.*

This wider angled panoramic view of the east end of the station, as seen from the western parapet of the overbridge which carries Holdenhurst Road across the railway, reveals Modified 'West Country' No. 35026 *Yes Tor* setting off for Waterloo with the 2.10pm (Sundays) from Bournemouth West. Another photographer has chosen the Down platform to take a 'going away' shot, prior to the locomotive disappearing from view into what, in effect, is a short tunnel. *22nd August 1965*

NEAR TALBOT WOODS

Another visit to the lineside at what Norman invariably described as '*near Talbot Woods*' but which some might describe as Talbot Heath. He took up a favoured position, looking due east from the cutting between the Rothesay Road and Glanferness Avenue overbridges.

BR 'Standard' Class 5 4-6-0 No. 73171 heads west towards Gas Works Junction with the 10.30am Waterloo-Weymouth. The overbridge is again the one carrying Glenferness Avenue and is still there but when last visited by this writer in the early-2000s, the lineside here was barely recognisable as being this same view, so many trees having grown along both sides of the cutting. *22nd August 1965*

'Merchant Navy' No. 35003 *Royal Mail* has slowed for adverse signals and is about to suffer the indignity of being brought to an unscheduled halt with the Down 'Bournemouth Belle', less than a couple of miles short of its destination. *10th October 1965*

PARKSTONE

BR Class '5' No. 73115 drifts downhill through Parkstone station with a Sundays Eastleigh to Weymouth service. The climb in the opposite (Up) direction commences at 1 in 60 about a mile to the east of Poole station and this extends for around three-quarters of a mile before stiffening to 1 in 50 for a further quarter-mile (the nadir of more than one steam-hauled special in recent times!). This precedes an easing to 1 in 300 through the platforms here before the grade reverts to 1 in 60 round a reverse curve for almost another half mile, prior to easing for the remainder of the incline to Branksome. The 4-6-0 has just passed onto the 1 in 50 downgrade and Norman's low-level camera position serves to accentuate the change from the much less severe gradient though the station.

The siding in the right foreground extended just behind the photographer's position. It was the location where an old tender, used at Bournemouth Central mpd to collect lime sludge from the water softening plant, was brought out to Parkstone and left for several days to enable the contents to drain out and be deposited down the side of the embankment!

SUNDAYS AT BOURNEMOUTH WEST

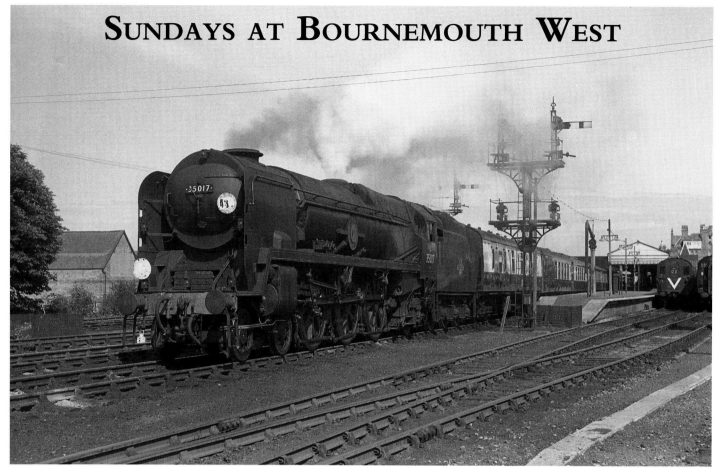

'Merchant Navy' No. 35017 *Belgian Marine* prepares to depart from Platform 4 with the 'Bournemouth Belle' Pullman train to Waterloo. A 'Hampshire' unit stands at Platform 3.

For so long the duty of 'M7' Class 0-4-4Ts, after the last of these finally succumbed in 1964, the task of station pilot duties usually fell to one of the Ivatt 2-6-2Ts, as per No. 41295. The duties were concerned almost entirely with the removal of empty stock from incoming services (much of which was hauled to the nearby mechanical washing plant for cleansing) and propelling stock into the alloted platform line to form an outgoing service. *22nd August 1965*

'Battle of Britain' Class No. 34064 *Fighter Command* sets off from Platform 5 with a Sunday service to Waterloo. *6th June 1965*
Having been returned to traffic in April 1962, following an overhaul which included fitting a Giesl oblong ejector and microspark arrestor, this locomotive was considered by many to be capable of duties usually the preserve of the more powerful 'Merchant Navy' Class, one of which can be seen waiting in the adjacent Platform 4. No. 34064 also held the distinction of being the 1,000th engine completed at Brighton Works, when released into traffic in July 1947.

ISLE OF WIGHT – 3

During the first three days in Octber 1965, Norman and Ivo paid a final visit to the Isle of Wight to photograph what had been scheduled to be the last three days of steam operation and – from the 4th October – closure of all but the Ryde Pier Head to Shanklin section. In the event, both the demise of steam and the closures were deferred because of delays in obtaining the necessary licences for the replacement bus services (just as was to occure on the S&D line three months later). As with the previous visits, the two photographers decided to limit their activities to the short section of line between Ryde St. Johns Road and Smallbrook Junction.

Plenty of enthusiasts in evidence on the 'last' Sunday, either travelling on board or merely watching from the platform as Class 'O2' 0-4-4T No. W26 *Whitwell* pulls away from Ryde St. Johns Road past the impressive signal box with a service bound for Newport and Cowes. *3rd October 1965 Note how, this time, all four dolls on the signal gantry carry an arm. This visit, unlike those previously made, was undertaken outside the summer period, so the lines towards Smallbrook were being worked as two single parallel lines to the next block post on both routes (to Brading on the Ventnor line and Havenstreet on the Newport line).*

The roof of Ryde St. Johns Road signal box can just be seen to the rear of this train to Ventnor, as No. W28 *Ashey* gathers speed after pausing at the station. Somebody has cleaned a small part of the front buffer beam to reveal the number of the locomotive. *3rd October 1965 The flat-roofed building, a part of which is just visible above the rear three coaches of the train and to the left of the signal box, is that of Ryde motive power depot.*

No. W28 *Ashey* features again with a Ventnor line service, this time immediately south of the overbridge which carries Smallbrook Lane across the railway.
1st October 1965
Note the two signal arms on a gantry attached to the bridge. These are the Up Distants for Ryde St. Johns Road, an indication that both lines from Smallbrook Junction were being operated as single lines. In the busy summer period, the right-hand arm was removed and this length of railway reverted to a double line block section. In plans come to fruition, the left-hand line seen here will one day be used by steam-hauled trains, as the popular Isle of Wight Steam Railway is hoping to extend from the present interchange platform at Smallbrook Junction to Ryde St. Johns Road station.

'Smile please'! All eyes appear to be watching Norman; perhaps it was his use of a large quarter-plate camera which caught their attention. No. W31 *Chale* looks somewhat travel weary in charge of a train to Newport and Cowes. The original nameplate had been removed and substituted by what appears to be a hand-painted effort on the side of the 0-4-4T. In 1966, the nameplates of all the remaining engines were removed for safekeeping and replaced by metal strips with letters hand-painted in yellow.
Steam on the island was eventually brought to an end by BR on 31st December 1966 and only the line from Ryde Pier Head to Shanklin was retained. It closed temporarily whilst a third-rail electric system was installed and former London Transport Underground stock was modified for use on the island.

'THE VECTIS FAREWELL' RAILTOUR

In anticipation of the end of steam–hauled services on the Isle of Wight, the Locomotive Club of Great Britain organised a railtour commencing from Waterloo on Sunday, 3rd October 1965. Class 'O2' 0-4-4T No. W24 *Calbourne* was 'spruced up' in preparation for two return journeys from Ryde Pier Head – the first to Cowes, the second to Ventnor.

This is the first journey setting off from Ryde St. Johns Road station *en route* to Newport and Cowes. The train was made up to six coaches.

For the second return journey, this time to Ventnor, No. W24 was joined by No. W14 *Fishbourne*, the latter also appearing in excellent external condition. Here the pair approach Smallbrook Junction, on the outward run. Note that No. W24 was minus its nameplates.

These locomotives were retained to work engineers trains in conjunction with the third-rail electrification project, following the completion of which both were withdrawn. In 1967, the Wight Locomotive Society purchased No. W24 Calbourne *from BR. It formed the first of the several locomotives which are today in the use or care of the Isle of Wight Steam Railway, now a major tourest attraction on Vectis. Despite the hope to save No. 14* Fishbourne, *she was not so fortunate and succumed to the scrapman's torch.*

The present-day Isle of Wight Steam Railway represents the efforts to date (2015) of more than four decades since it first commenced running steam-hauled trains over the first 1½ miles between Havenstreet and Wootton, extended in 1991 to the present 5 miles between Wootton and Smallbrook Junction.

SOUTHAMPTON CENTRAL – A FINAL VISIT

To complete his 'photographic season' for 1965, Norman returned to Southampton Central; in fact this image appears to be the last of many photographs (both monochrome and colour transparency) taken here by Norman. It is rather appropriate that the motive power is 'West Country' Class No. 34023 *Blackmore Vale*, the first example of an unrebuilt Bulleid 'light Pacific' to be purchased for restoration. Having just taken on water, she is seen here waiting to depart with the 11.00am Bournemouth West-Waterloo. *6th October 1965*

No. 34023 was purchased from BR for £1,900 by the Bulleid Locomotive Society and transferred to Longmoor. Following the closure of this former military railway site and a short stay at Liss, the society (known by then as the Bulleid Society Ltd) moved the locomotive to the Bluebell Railway, which has been its base ever since. Currently (2015), No. 34023, is on static display at Sheffield Park pending a further major overhaul and repair, having seen many more years in active service since this picture was taken. The Up side buildings at Southampton Central, including the impressive 100ft clock tower erected in 1892, were demolished late in 1966 prior to the redevelopment of that side of the station, which included a five-story flat-roofed station-cum-office block known now as 'Overline House'.

Norman and Ivo obtained their first photographs of the 'Dorset Belle' Special as it approached the station at Hamworthy Junction, between Poole and Wareham. However, just as Norman pressed the button, the blustery wind caught the exhust with the result seen.

'THE DORSET BELLE'

A trip along the branch line to Swanage and back (No. 35028 having handed over to Ivatt 2-6-2Ts No's 41284 and 41301 for this part of the itinerary) enabled Ivo and Norman to 'leap-frog' ahead of the Special. They thus had plenty of time to be ready to take this next view of No. 35028 on the final stage of the outward run from Wareham to Weymouth. Here, as it approaches Wool station, this time an unobstructed view of the train was achieved.

The return journey commenced with the two BR-Built Ivatt tanks in charge from Weymouth to Maiden Newton. No. 41301 was about to be transferred onto the rear of the Special, prior to making a 'top and tail' journey along the branch line to Bridport and back.

SECTION 6
1966-67

Norman's and Ivo's visits to various Southern Region lineside locations during 1966 were undertaken with the objective of photographing more of the many 'specials', most of which were organised by various enthusiasts' clubs. They also made just the occasional foray to witness both the remnants and final fling of public steam-hauled services on the main line near Weymouth, plus a last visit to the Swanage Branch was fitted in.

'The Dorset Belle' was a railtour organised by the Locomotive Club of Great Britain and ran on Sunday 27th February 1966. Motive power from Waterloo to Weymouth was provided by 'Merchant Navy' Class No. 35028 *Clan Line*. The outward tour was routed via Woking, Alton and 'over the Alps' to Arlesford; then Winchester, Eastleigh, Southampton, Bournemouth, Poole and Wareham.

After a trip along the Swanage Branch, the Special made for Weymouth. Here it reversed direction and was taken over by two Ivatt 2-6-2 tanks to run via Dorchester West to Maiden Newton, for the Bridport Branch. On returning to Maiden Newton and having undertaken another reversal, the tour continued behind the two tanks to Yeovil Pen Mill, then regained the main line at Yeovil Junction; this leg of the journey required two further reversals. From Yeovil Junction, No. 34057 *Biggin Hill* returned the Special to Waterloo, via Salisbury, Basingstoke and Woking.

SOMERSET & DORSET RAILTOURS

Six days after 'The Dorset Belle' railtour, another Special organised by the LCGB ran, with No. 35028 in charge for much of the itinerary. This was the 'Somerset & Dorset Rail Tour' on Saturday 5th March 1966, the last day of public services over the much loved S&D line.

Clan Line headed the Special from Waterloo, via Salisbury to Templecombe and is seen here approaching Buckhorn Weston Tunnel. Following arrival at Templecombe, the tour traversed the S&D line to Highbridge and returned to Evercreech Junction. Next came a run across the Mendips to Bath Green Park, then all the way south to Bournemouth Central. The legs over the S&D were hauled by other locomotives, whilst No. 35028 ran 'light engine' to Bournemouth in order to return the train back to Waterloo.

On the following day, Sunday 6th March 1966, two final S&D tours were organised. The Midland Area of the Stephenson Locomotive Society (SLS) ran a DMU to Bath Green Park, connecting into a run to Bournemouth Central and return behind Class '8F' 2-8-0 No. 48706 and BR 'Standard 4' Class 2-6-4T No. 80043. But a more diverse itinerary was provided with the other Special train, organised by the RCTS. This used No. 35028 again, commencing from Waterloo and running to Bournemouth via Staines, Virginia Water, Aldershot and the Alton to Winchester route. No. 35028 remained in charge of the Special from Bournemouth and along the S&D from Broadstone as far as Templecombe Junction, thus defying a route ban for the 'Merchant Navy' Class over the S&D but, by this final weekend, nobody cared any more about such rules! Norman took this photograph as the train approached Templecombe from the south.

Being 'otherwise engaged' with his annual – and essential – Royal Observer Corps exams, Ivo Peters managed only to get to the S&D lineside near Cole late on the Saturday afternoon. So we think Norman was in the company of another excellent photographer, Derek Cross, on this occasion.

From Templecombe (former No. 2) Junction to Highbridge, the Special was hauled by a pair of Ivatt 2-6-2Ts, No's 41283 and 41249. At Highbridge, with the passengers temporarily 'detrained', the stock was transferred onto the WR Bristol-Taunton main line for the next leg of the journey. This saw No. 34013 *Okehampton* in charge for the run through Bristol and over the former Midland route as far as Mangotsfield North Junction. Norman photographed No. 34013 accelerating the Special northwards from Highbridge.

'THE NEW FORESTER'

'Q1' Class 0-6-0 No. 33006 at Lymington Pier, in the process of running round the stock forming 'The New Forester Rail Tour' on 19th March 1966. This was another Special organised by the LCGB.

Officially, No. 33006 – the last active member of this class – had been withdrawn, from Guildford, on 9th January 1966. However, it was retained for railtour use and, in addition to the Special seen here, also worked the 'Wilts & Hants' tour train (see opposite) on 3rd April. The locomotive was sold to Cashmores of Newport and, some time after the April tour was moved from Nine Elms to Feltham for stabling (storage). Eventually it left for Newport with Class 'S15' No. 30837 on 27th June but it appears that something must have gone awry because both were noted at Gloucester on 20th July and 4th August. Eventually, it was taken into the breaker's yard at Newport on 13th August 1966.

No. 33006, about to cross the Lymington River on the approach to Lymington Town station, with the return run along the branch prior to regaining the main line at Brokenhurst.

'THE WILTS & HANTS' RAILTOUR

No. 33006 together with 'U' Class 2-6-0 No. 31639 (the 'Q1' having taken over from No. 31411 at Salisbury) head the 'Wilts & Hants' Special southwards from Romsey towards Southampton on 3rd April 1966. Yet another railtour organised by the RCTS, the trip had commenced from and would return to Waterloo. *We think this scene might have been photographed from the A27 Southampton Road overbridge near Ashfield. Norman gave no clue!*

MICHELDEVER

On Spring Bank Holiday 1966 (the last Monday in May), Norman accompanied Ivo in the Bentley eastwards along the A303, before turning off to reach the lineside just to the south of Micheldever station. As far as can be ascertained, Norman took only two photographs, both from the same position and both featuring Down trains. The first is featured here and shows BR 'Standard' Class '5' No. 73069 with a Waterloo-Weymouth service. The picture includes our first sighting in this tome of what appears to be the (then) newly adopted British Railways blue and grey livery, as applied to the second and third coaches. *30th May 1966*

SWANAGE BRANCH

Summer 1966 was to witness the final few months of regular steam operation over the branch line to Swanage. From 5th September, 'Hampshire' diesel-electric multiple units took over and this heralded the start of reducing the ten miles from Worgret Junction to a 'basic railway' and eventual closure.

In the final few years of steam over the Swanage Branch, BR Standard Class '4' 2-6-0s became a regular sight and none more so than No. 76010, which was destined to work the final steam hauled, state controlled passenger service* from Swanage on 4th September 1966. Just five weeks earlier, No. 76010 pulls away from the seaside terminus, passing the small engine shed, with the 12.52pm (Sundays) to Wareham. *31st July 1966*
Had to be careful how this was phrased – in the summer of 1966 who, in their wildest imagination, would have thought that a half-century later it is possible to travel to Swanage behind steam once again!

Later on the same day, No. 76010 is featured again, now working the 2.25pm (Sundays) service from Swanage. The engine is seen here climbing beyond the outskirts of the town near Washpond Lane, Herston. *31st July 1966*

'THE GREEN ARROW' RAILTOUR

Another Peters/Lockett joint visit, this time to the lineside near Stowell, about a mile west of Templecombe. Their objective was to photograph an ex-L.&NER Class 'V2' 2-6-2, which had been requested as motive power by the LCGB for the 'Green Arrow' railtour for at least a part of a run from Waterloo to Weymouth, via Yeovil, then returning to the capital via Bournemouth and Southampton. The two photographers (and doubtless many others) were to be disappointed! The locomotive, No. 60919, had been brought south from Dundee to work the tour but failed and was replaced by Stanier Class '5' 4-6-0 No. 45493, seen here ahead of rebuilt 'West Country' No. 34100 *Appledore* as they emerge from a deep cutting and complete the climb from the Cale Valley. *3rd July 1966*

Whilst the Special was involved with a double reversal at Yeovil – first at the Junction station, then at Pen Mill – the two photographers had more than enough time to get to this next vantage point at the northern end of Evershot Tunnel. The train is about to enter the 308 yds-long tunnel, nearing the end of six miles of adverse gradients which lifted the line out of the Yeo Valley. The climb culminated with nearly two miles at 1 in 51.

At Weymouth, the tour included a trip along the 'tramway' to the quay behind Ivatt 2-6-2T No. 41298. The return from Weymouth Town station towards Waterloo saw No. 45493 partnered by unrebuilt 'West Country' No. 34002 *Salisbury*, which – appropriately – had brought the train unaided on the initial leg from Waterloo as far west as the city after which the 4-6-2 was named. Norman and Ivo both photogaphed the Special for a third and final time as it climbed the 1 in 50 on the approach to Upway Wishing Well Halt and Bincombe Tunnels.

CLIMBING TOWARDS
UPWAY WISHING WELL HALT

A pair of BR 'Standards', Class '4' 2-6-0 No. 76026 assisting Class '5' 4-6-0 No. 73018, on the climb towards Upway Wishing Well Halt with the 3.50pm Weymouth to Waterloo. *20th August 1966*
Note the large hoarding in the foreground, positioned to attract the attention of motorists using the (then) busy Weymouth-Dorchester main road (on a section nowadays 'by-passed' by means of the Weymouth Relief Road). For several years from around 1960, the hoarding carried a very prominent advertisement urging motorists to 'Put a tiger in your tank' by purchasing 'Esso Extra' petrol; surely amongst the best remembered and most successful advertising campaigns ever mounted.

Here on the four-mile climb up from Weymouth, modified 'West Country' Class No. 34004 *Yeovil* is assisted by Type 3 diesel-electric locomotive No. D6510 with the 6.15pm Weymouth to Waterloo train. This severe climb culminates with 1¼ miles at 1 in 50 to Upway Wishing Well Halt, easing only slightly to 1 in 52 for the passage through the tunnels at Bincombe, before reaching the summit. *20th August 1966*
No. D6510 was allocated to Eastleigh at the date of this photograph. The Type 3 (subsequently Class '33') 'Cromptons' were destined to become a very familiar sight on the Bournemouth-Weymouth route following electrification from Waterloo to Bournemouth. At the latter station, the trains were divided and a Class '33' attached to haul the coaching stock destined for Weymouth. In the reverse direction, the locomotive propelled its stock from Weymouth to Bournemouth.

A 'BLACK FIVE' INTERLOPER

Wolverhampton Oxley-based Stanier Class '5' 4-6-0, No. 44856 crosses the heathlands west of Lymington and heads towards Sway with the 10.06am York to Poole. Note the '2B' shed code stencilled onto the smokebox door; since September 1963, this former Nuneaton shed code had been reassigned to Oxley. *30th May 1966*

The regular use of 'Black Fives' for this and the corresponding Up service between Poole and Banbury, survived for about eight months during 1966, until 3rd September, when through running via the Great Central line was brought to an end.

A visit to Salisbury motive power depot found modified 'West Country' Class No. 34013 *Okehampton* resting between duties at what had been its home for the past three years and, indeed, its final allocation. Maintained in excellent external condition, this locomotive had become a favourite choice for a number of railtours. When pictured here, she had only just recently received a final 'Light Casual' overhaul. *14th August 1966*

SARUM SPECIALS

A month later, Norman and Ivo visited Salisbury again, this time to photograph the 'Flying Scotsman Goes South' Special. The privately-restored No. 4472 worked this train from London (Victoria) to Brighton and Eastleigh, where these two BR Standard Class '4' 2-6-4Ts, No's 80152 and 80016, took over for a run across to Salisbury and back. On return to Eastleigh, No. 4472 worked the train back via Brighton to London. In this first view, the Special, organised by 'Locomotive Preservation (Southern) Ltd' has just emerged from Salisbury Tunnel at a location where, since the late-1960s, the railway has been bridged by Churchill Way North, a part of the Salisbury inner relief road. *17th September 1966*

Both locomotives were turned at Salisbury mpd and having just commenced the return leg to Eastleigh, emerge with the Special from the opposite end of Salisbury Tunnel to that featured in the upper view, to take the Romsey line at Tunnel Junction.

It is conjecture as to whether Norman had gone to Salisbury in anticipation of photographing the restored No. 4472 at the head of this Special, only to be surprised by the appearance of a pair of 'Standard' 2-6-4Ts. The lower scene was also photographed by Ivo Peters, so he and Norman will have travelled together and there is no evidence of them proceeding farther south-east to photograph No. 4472 in the vicinity of Eastleigh.

'THE BRIDPORT BELLE' – WHAT A TOUR!

On 22nd January 1967, the LCGB organised the 'Bridport Belle' railtour, which was effectively a repeat of the successful 'Dorset Belle' tour undertaken the previous February. This one, however, was to become infamous for all the unplanned events, which included the discovery of a dead body in a carriage toilet, apparently remaining from when the stock had been used the previous day! Reportedly, the body was removed during a seven minute special stop at Basingstoke, following which the tour continued on its way. One cannot imagine such an occurrence being dealt with in this casual manner today.

The Special later visited the Bridport Branch and, again in a repeat of the tour in February 1966 (*see pages 140 and 141*), a pair of Ivatt 2-6-2Ts were used for the return trip from Maiden Newton. However, on this occasion – and to add insult to the earlier problem – the Special, 'topped and tailed' by No's 41295 and 41320, stalled in the rain on the steep incline of Loders Bank during the return run. After several failed attempts to restart, No. 41320, now in need of water, ran light back to the main line where assistance was requested. This arrived from Weymouth in the form of a Type 3 'Crompton' diesel which rescued the 'Bridport Belle' and No. 41295 on the rear.

This pair of 'light Pacifics', No's 34057 *Biggin Hill* and 34102 *Lapford*, were used for the initial and final stages of the tour, between Waterloo to Salisbury and return. Despite the late running, a stop was included here at the site of the goods yard just short of Grateley station, where seemingly most of the passengers eagerly detrained, apparently in order to photograph a run-past.

OPPOSITE PAGE TOP: Hopefully with all safely back on board, the Special got underway again amid much evidence of rationalisation of the infrastructure at Grateley station. Despite this, however, Grateley signal box was still in use, finally closing on 2nd May 1968.
Grateley signal box was interesting, opening in July 1901 and being an experimental installation by the L&SWR of low pressure pneumatic signalling. It controlled a series of automatic signals installed between Grateley and Andover Junction. Note the unusual bay window lookout, provided so that the signalman could see the farthest set of points during shunting operations (the goods yard was at the other end of the station), as there was no indicator for the track circuits inside the box. A conventional mechanical frame replaced the experimental one in 1921.

OPPOSITE PAGE BOTTOM: At Salisbury, No. 34102 was removed leaving No. 34057 *Biggin Hill* in sole charge of the next leg of the tour, along the Wylye Valley to Westbury. Here the Special approaches the road overbridge near Sherrington.

NEAR RADIPOLE

Mention was made a few pages earlier of the taxing four-mile climb faced by trains when heading away from Weymouth. The location seen here is much closer to the town, on the somewhat easier gradients near Radipole Halt. A very presentable No. 34108 *Wincanton*, with a surplus of steam, descends towards the terminus with the Weymouth portion of the 1.30pm from Waterloo. Radipole Halt can be seen just to the rear of the train. *27th March 1967*
The skyline in the distance gives an idea of how much the railway has to climb from Weymouth before passing through the tunnels at Binscombe and reaching the summit cutting.

As the late-afternoon shadows lengthen, BR 'Standard' Class '5' No. 73029 heads away from the terminus with what Norman described as the second part of the 5.30pm Weymouth to Waterloo. There does not appear to be a plume of exhaust above the rear of the train, so presumably the loading was such that a banker was considered unnecessary. *27th March 1967*

With a blustery wind blowing in from the sea and snatching away the exhaust, No. 34008 *Padstow* gets to grips with a heavy Channel Island Boat Train bound for Waterloo. A second, impressive, exhaust seen above the rear of the train confirms that assistance was being provided on this occasion. *27th March 1967*

'THE HAMPSHIRE BRANCH LINES' RAILTOUR

On 9th April 1967, Norman and Ivo set out to photograph yet another trip organised by the RCTS, 'The Hampshire Branch Lines' railtour. The first leg from Waterloo was hauled by 'Merchant Navy' No. 35023 *Holland-Afrika Line*, here travelling downhill at speed and still some miles to the north-east of Salisbury, where the 4-6-2 would be replaced.

The fireman can be seen holding on to his cap, whilst the enthusiast leaning from the carriage window, doubtless to savour the performance of the engine, is wearing an essential item – a large pair of leather cased goggles! Such details only become fully apparent when the digital image is considerably enlarged.

A well-presented No. 34057 *Biggin Hill* (although lacking various adornments) was in charge of the next leg of the journey, to Southampton. Whilst the train changed locomotives at Salisbury, the two photographers easily got ahead, first to capture it near West Grimstead, a few miles to the west of the city, then again here, at the lineside near Chandlers Ford, between Romsey and Eastleigh.

This pair of 'USA' Class 0-6-0Ts, No's 30069 and 30064, took over the Special at Southampton for a trip over the branch to Fawley. Here (above) the two locomotives, coupled bunker to bunker, are seen near Dibden on the outward leg. On the return trip (below) to the Southampton-Bournemouth main line at Totton, the Special passes through a wooded section near Marchwood with No. 30064 now leading.

'DORSET COAST EXPRESS'

This LCGB railtour, made up of ten coaches, ran from Waterloo on 7th May 1967 and visited the Swanage Branch and Weymouth. No. 34021 *Dartmoor* had been in charge since leaving London and travelled via Guildford, Havant, Fareham and Southampton. At Wareham, No. 34023 *Blackmore Vale* took charge of the train for two return trips over the Swanage Branch, on which all passenger services had been operated by 'Hampshire' diesel-electric multiple units from 5th September the previous year. BR Class '4' 2-6-4T No. 80011 was attached to the rear of the Special for the two return journeys across the Isle of Purbeck. Here the train is seen crossing Corfe Common.

The Special at Swanage, where many of the photographers detrained. The attractive signal box remained in operation but only for one more month, being closed from 6th June 1967, then later demolished.
Since 2003, there has been an impressive replacement signal box located on the opposite side of the line, built in the same style (although with a larger 'footprint') for the much admired and extremely popular Swanage Railway which operates the rebuilt line, 7 miles of which were torn up with indecent haste after the last public service ran on 1st January 1972.

Now making a return run to Wareham, No. 80011 leads the Special across Corfe Viaduct on the climb towards Nordon, with No. 34023 *Blackmore Vale* bringing up the rear of the train.

'HOME & AWAY' NEAR WEYMOUTH

The 'Dorset Coast Express', as featured on the previous two pages, made its way from Wareham to Weymouth behind No. 34023 *Blackmore Vale*. Norman merely logged this location as '*near Weymouth*' but the changes around here have been so great that I cannot place it. I suspect the same scene today will include the Weymouth Relief Road, which parallels the Down side of the railway. *7th May 1967*

Having only recently been restored to the former L&NER Blue livery, Class 'A4' No. 4498 *Sir Nigel Gresley* was used for the 'On tour in the South' two-day Special organised by the A4 Locomotive Society. On this, the second day, No. 4498 heads out of Weymouth at the start of the return to Waterloo. A trail of exhaust at the rear confirms the 'A4' is receiving hearty assistance 'up the bank', apparently provided by 'Battle of Britain' No. 34087 *145 Squadron*. *4th June 1967*
The A4 had just crossed Chapel Lane, Broadway; the detached house prominent on the left – known as 'Coombe Farm' – can still be seen in 2015.

FAREWELL TO STEAM SPECIALS

The fast approaching and well-publicised demise of steam motive power on the Southern Region prompted the promotion of all manner of 'farewell' special trains. Two such excursions were the Warwickshire Railway Society's 'Farewell to Steam on the LSWR' on 11th June 1967 and the RCTS organised 'Farewell to Southern Steam' which ran just seven days later.

This is the WRS rail tour, which started from Birmingham for a visit of the former L&SWR main line, to which access had been gained via Willisden Junction and Clapham Junction. The tour included a visit to the Swanage Branch. Rebuilt 'West Country' Class No. 34004 *Yeovil*, with BR 'Standard' Class '4' 2-6-4T No. 80146 bringing up the rear, is about to pass under the road bridge at Afflington, with Corfe Castle prominent on the skyline.

No. 34004 *Yeovil* took the 'Farewell to Steam on the LSWR' Special forward from Wareham to Dorchester and Weymouth. The train is seen here passing through the heathland near Moredon, east of Dorchester.

As will be noticed, some locomotives were no longer carrying a smokebox numberplate, whilst of those formerly 'named', more and more examples were now running without nameplates. Within these pages, the name will continue to be given irrespective of whether it was still carried.

THE RCTS
'FAREWELL TO SOUTHERN STEAM' RAILTOUR

The RCTS 'Farewell to Southern Steam' railtour, which ran on 18th June 1967, commenced from and returned to Waterloo. This too covered the line to Weymouth and included a foray over the Swanage Branch, the last BR steam-hauled train to visit the Isle of Purbeck line. By this date, Norman had been making more use of 35mm colour transparency film. Consequently, he took only two monochrome photographs of the RCTS railtour. This, the first, is of No. 34089 *602 Squadron* which, having arrived at Weymouth on the leg from Wareham, retired to the mpd to be turned.

THE NORMAN LOCKETT ARCHIVE

165

For the first part of the return journey, via Bournemouth and Eastleigh to Salisbury, the motive power was provided by No. 34023 *Blackmoor Vale* assisting No. 34108 *Wincanton*. The latter had piloted the train on an earlier leg of the tour from Southampton to Wareham, from where it travelled 'light' to Weymouth. Seen here, the train has just left the terminus and is approaching Radipole Halt where a stop was to be made. According to a report in *The Railway Observer* (September 1967), the Special called at Radipole Halt on both the inwards and return journeys, specifically to offload and later collect those passengers who had expressed the wish to visit Weymouth mpd. Perhaps it was two of those enthusiasts who can be seen in the previous photograph helping to turn No. 34089 at the depot. The Special was now running about 35 minutes late, because on arrival at Weymouth a 'hot box' had been discovered on one of the coaches. This had to be removed and a replacement vehicle found.

BR 'FAREWELL TO SOUTHERN STEAM' SPECIALS

This, the first of two Specials run by BR Southern Region on Sunday, 2nd July 1967, was headed in both directions between Waterloo and Weymouth by 'Merchant Navy' Class No. 35008 *Orient Line*. Norman photographed No. 35008 heading westwards at speed through the New Forest, between Woodfidley Crossing and Brockenhurst. The locomotive was reported as having put up an excellent performance with speeds reaching 90mph. No. 35008 was assisted between Weymouth and Bournemouth on the return run by No. 35007 *Aberdeen Commonwealth*

The other BR Special ran from Waterloo to Bournemouth and back behind No. 35028 *Clan Line*.
This scene features the early part of the return journey, running eastwards along the same section of line as featured above; the Special is approaching the curve past Woodfidley Crossing, heading towards Beaulieu Road station. Notice the couple enjoying a lineside picnic!

LAST LINESIDE VISITS

Having photographed the 'Farewell to Southern Steam' Specials, Norman made four more visits to south Dorset on consecutive days, from 4th to 7th July. On the second day, 5th July, Norman travelled with Ivo and all of their photographs appear to have been taken at Bincombe. It is reasonable to assume that they clambered down into the cutting between the two tunnels and, discovering no others had done likewise, decided to 'stay put'. On the other three days, Norman – reliant on public transport – opted to return to a location on the outskirts of Weymouth, just a little south of Radipole Halt and immediately to the north of the 'Jersey Sidings'. Again, he appears to have struck lucky in selecting somewhere that was not over-run by other lineside observers. So, he ventured no closer towards the terminus at Weymouth to take his final photographs featuring Southern Region steam-hauled services. Future visits to photograph what remained of BR main line steam would involve far longer journeys to remote lineside locations more than 250 miles removed from the South Coast of England.★

'Merchant Navy' Class No. 35023 *Holland-Afrika Line* emerges from the shorter of the two tunnels at Bincombe with the 5.30pm Weymouth to Waterloo. Note the use of lamps rather than discs to signify the route of the train. *5th July 1967*

Ivo Peters can be seen closer to the northern portal of what is the shorter of the two tunnels at Bincombe. The Dorchester-Weymouth road (A354) passed over this tunnel before descending around a hairpin bend and heading under the railway. Within that short length of railway was situated Upway Wishing Well Halt (closed in 1957). Nowadays, the A345 hereabouts is the 4½ mile-long Weymouth Relief Road; a scheme first proposed in 1948 and opened in 2011, just in time for those visiting Weymouth and Portland for the 2012 Olympic and Paralympic Games sailing events. I don't recall any upgrade to the railway for the same purpose, other than some long-overdue improvements to Weymouth station.

*That's just a 'tease' for a future book in this series of albums!

Turning to look in the opposite direction to that seen in the previous photograph, BR Class '4' 2-6-0 No. 76005 has just emerged from the longer (814 yards) of the two tunnels with a lengthy freight. This includes a sizeable head of empty vans used for the perishables traffic received at Weymouth from the Channel islands. *5th July 1967*
Note that Ivo had again decided to take up a position much nearer the portal of the tunnel, as he had done in the previous image with the other tunnel mouth.

BR Class '4' 2-6-4T No. 80146 climbs the 1 in 52 grade with the 5.00pm parcels train from Weymouth. The Up platform of the (already closed) Upway Wishing Well Halt is just visible beyond the tunnel. *5th July 1967*
As its name indicates, Upwey Wishing Well Halt was provided for the benefit of visitors to the nearby wishing well and opened on 28th May 1905. The well is a natural spring and source of the River Wey. Visited on several occasions by George III, the waters are said to have healing properties but the wishing well aspect dates only from the early 20th century, being started as a visitor attraction. The halt was closed on 7th January 1957.

Other than the absence of the nameplate, 'Merchant Navy' No. 35007 *Aberdeen Commonwealth* did not give the impression of a locomotive destined to make just two more revenue earning journeys. Here she climbs between the two tunnels with the 5.41pm Weymouth to Bournemouth service. *5th July 1967*
It became no secret that many of the footplate crews were, within the overall bounds of safety, 'throwing caution to the winds' with their final few runs in charge of these steam hauled trains. On the day after Norman took this photograph, No. 35007 reportedly reached 98mph before a partial failure at Brookwood – a broken inside cylinder cover – put an end to such speeds. Despite this, the 'Pacific' with its train succeeded in reaching Waterloo before retiring to Nine Elms mpd, from where it was withdrawn and stored awaiting sale for scrap.

BR Class '4' 2-6-0 No. 76026, in charge of a mixed freight, cautiously approaches the end of her run on the descent past **Radipole Halt**. *6th July 1967 Radipole Halt was opened on 1st July 1905, at a time when the GWR were opening numerous such stopping places across their system following the succesful introduction of steam railmotor services. The official closure date of this halt is recorded as 6th February 1984. However, the last trains called there on New Year's Eve 1983, after which the platforms were considered to have become unsafe for further use.*

At 2.45pm, BR Class '5' No. 73018, with a heavily loaded Weymouth-Westbury 'Perisher', climbs past the buffer stops protecting the ends of the three long 'Jersey Sidings' which feature in several of these views. *6th July 1967*
When the writer last visited Weymouth by train a few years ago, two of the 'Jersey Sidings' were still in place. Their continued use apparently includes the stabling of stock from visiting steam hauled specials.

An Up parcels train climbs towards Radipole Halt. The number of the BR Class '4' 2-6-4T was not recorded by Norman but is thought to be No. 80011. Norman noted the time as 5.05pm, so this is most likely a 5.00pm departure from Weymouth. *7th July 1967*

THE FINAL IMAGE

This is Norman Lockett's final photograph depicting BR Southern Region Steam. Modified 'West Country' No. 34013 *Okehampton*, now looking somewhat jaded since we last featured this locomotive whilst 'on shed' at Salisbury during the previous August, climbs away from Weymouth with the 5.30pm service to Waterloo. *Taken at 5.34pm on Thursday 7th July 1967*

It was perhaps rather appropriate that this particular Bulleid 'light Pacific' should be the last example to be photographed by Norman during the final few days of Southern steam, for it had been this same locomotive, albeit in its unrebuilt form, that he captured on a glass-plate negative during one of his earliest post-war visits to the lineside, and which is reproduced across pages 2 and 3 of this volume.